Intermediate Student's Book

# New Headway

## English Course

Part B Units 7–12

**Liz & John Soars**

Oxford University Press 1996

# Contents

# SKILLS DEVELOPMENT

# The world of work

## Present Perfect active and passive
## On the telephone

---

## 7

**Test your grammar**

**1** Work in pairs. Ask and answer the questions.

a What do you do?
b How long have you had your present job?
c What did you do before that?
d

Do you live in a house or a flat?

e How long have you lived there?
f When did you move there?
g How long have you known your teacher?
h When did you first meet your teacher?
i Have you ever been to America?
j If so, when did you go?

**2** Tell the rest of the class about your partner.

**3** There are three tenses used in the questions. What are they?

## PRESENTATION (1)

### Present Perfect Simple

1 Read the job advertisement. Does this job interest you? Do you have any of the necessary qualifications to apply?

# WORLDWATCH

**Business journalist** £35,000 p.a.

This international business magazine, with 23,000 readers worldwide, requires a journalist to help cover political news in Europe.

The successful applicant will be based in Geneva and should:

- have at least two years' experience in business journalism
- be fluent in French and German, and if possible have some knowledge of Spanish
- have a degree in politics
- have travelled widely.

Please write with full CV to
David Benton, *Worldwatch UK Ltd*,
357 Ferry Rd, Basingstoke RG2 5HP

WORLDWATCH

2 **T.48** Nancy Mann has applied for the job and is being interviewed. Listen to the interview. Do you think she will get the job?

3 Read the first part of Nancy's interview. Put the correct auxiliary verb *do*, *did*, or *have* into each gap.

I   Who _____ you work for at the moment, Ms Mann?

N   I work for the BBC World Service.

I   And how long _____ you worked for the BBC?

N   I _____ been with the BBC for five years. Yes, exactly five years.

I   And how long _____ you been their German correspondent?

N   For two years.

I   And what _____ you do before the BBC?

N   I worked as an interpreter for the EU.

Listen to the first part again and check your answers.

● Grammar questions

– Does she still work for the BBC?
– Does she still work for the EU?
– Explain why Nancy says:

*I **work** for the BBC World Service.*
*I've **worked** for them for five years.*
*I **worked** as an interpreter for the EU.*

4 Read and complete the second part of Nancy's interview with *did*, *was*, or *have*.

I   As you know, this job is based in Geneva. _____ you ever lived abroad before?

N   Oh yes, yes I _____ .

I   And when _____ you live abroad?

N   Well, in fact I _____ born in Argentina and I lived there until I was eleven. Also, I lived and worked in Brussels for two years when I _____ working for the EU.

I   That's interesting. _____ you travelled much?

N   Oh yes, yes indeed. I _____ travelled all over western and eastern Europe, and I _____ also been to many parts of South America.

I   And why _____ you go to these places?

N   Well, mostly for pleasure, but three years ago I went back to Argentina to cover various political stories in Buenos Aires for the BBC.

Listen and check your answers.

● Grammar question

– The interviewer asks:

*__Have__ you ever **lived** abroad?*
*When **did** you **live** abroad?*

Nancy says:
*I've **been** to many parts of South America.*
*... three years ago I **went** back to Argentina ...*

Why are different tenses used?

## PRACTICE

### 1 Biographies

1 Here are some more events from Nancy Mann's life. Match a line in **A** with a time expression in **B** to tell the story of her life. Put a letter a–k in the box.

**A**

a  She was born
b  She went to boarding school in England
c  She studied French and German
d  She hasn't spoken Spanish
e  She's worked in both eastern and western Europe
f  She worked in Brussels
g  She's worked for the BBC
h  She hasn't worked abroad
i  She married for the first time
j  She's been married
k  She married for the third time

**B**

☐ for the last five years.
☐ three times.
☐ from 1970 to 1977.
☐ *e* at various times in her life.
☐ when she was twenty-one.
☐ when she was at Oxford University.
☐ *a* in Argentina in 1959.
☐ for two years, from 1989 to 1991.
☐ last year.
☐ since her son was born four years ago.
☐ since she was in Buenos Aires three years ago.

2   **T.49**   Listen and check your answers.

3 Work in pairs. Write similar tables of your own life. Ask your partner to match the events and the times to tell the story of your life. Correct any wrong times.

## 2 Time expressions

Put *for*, *since*, *in*, or *ago* into each gap.

a I was born _____ 1961.
b I went to university _____ three years.
c I passed my driving test fifteen years _____ .
d I've had a car _____ 1983.
e Now I've got a BMW. I've had it _____ two years.
f I met my wife _____ 1985.
g We've been married _____ nine years.
h Our first daughter was born six years _____ .
i We've lived in the same house _____ 1990.

## 3 *Have you ever ...?*

1 The following verbs are *all* irregular. What is the past simple and past participle?

| have | eat | win | forget | bring | make |
|------|------|------|--------|-------|------|
| be | drink | lose | sleep | find | give |
| meet | write | drive | hear | sing | |
| leave | read | ride | see | go (Careful!) | |

2 Work with a partner. Choose from the list and make dialogues like the example.

Example
be/America?

A *Have you ever been to America?*
B *Yes, I have./No, I haven't. I've never been there.*
A *When did you go?*
B *Two years ago. I went to Disneyland with my family.*

| | |
|---|---|
| have/an operation? | win/a competition? |
| be/on TV? | lose/your job? |
| write/a love letter? | hear/an opera? |
| ride/a motor bike? | see/a horror movie? |
| have/an English breakfast? | forget/an important birthday? |
| try/iced tea? | sleep/in the open air? |
| drive/a van? | sing/in a choir? |
| read/a book in a foreign language? | meet/anyone famous? |

3 Tell the class as much as you can remember about your partner.

## PRESENTATION (2)

### Present Perfect active and passive

1 Read the newspaper headlines. Check any new words.

a **DANGEROUS PRISONER ESCAPES**

b **Floods bring road chaos**

c **Kidnapped baby found**

d **US CAR WORKERS MADE REDUNDANT**

2 **T.50a** Read and listen to the radio news headlines of the same stories. Fill in the gaps with the exact words you hear.

Here is the news...

### RADIO NEWS HEADLINES

a The murderer Bruce Braden _____ from Parkhurst Prison on the Isle of Wight.
b After the heavy rain of the last few days, floods _____ chaos to drivers in the West Country.
c Amy Carter, the kidnapped baby from Leeds, _____ safe and well in a car park in Manchester.
d Two thousand car workers from a US car factory _____ redundant.

### ● Grammar questions

– Which of these questions can you answer? Which can't you answer?

*Who has escaped from prison?*
*What has brought chaos to the West Country?*
*Who has found Amy Carter?*
*Who has made the car workers redundant?*

– What is the difference between the verb forms in Exercise 2?

3  **T.50b**  Listen to the news items and fill in the gaps to complete the stories. What other information do you learn about each one?

a  Last night, the murderer Bruce Braden _____ from Parkhurst Prison. Prison officers _____ his cell empty at six o'clock this morning.

b  Early this morning, floods _____ chaos to many roads in Devon. Drivers left their cars and _____ to work through the flood water.

c  Late last night, the kidnapped baby Amy Carter, _____ safe and well in a car park in the centre of Manchester. The car park attendant _____ a noise coming from a rubbish bin and he _____ Amy wrapped in a warm blanket.

d  Two thousand car workers from the General Motors factory in Detroit _____ redundant yesterday. The management _____ them no warning. The men were shocked and furious when they _____ the news yesterday evening.

● Grammar questions

–  Which tense is used in the full stories in Exercise 3 above? Why?

–  Which tense is used in the headlines in Exercise 2 on page 67? Why?

## PRACTICE

### 1 Here is the news!

Work in pairs.

1  Here are some more headlines from newspapers. Make them into radio news headlines.

Examples

# Plane crashes in Colombia

*A Boeing 727 has crashed in the mountains of Colombia near Bogotá.*

## DANGEROUS PRISONER RECAPTURED

*The murderer Bruce Braden has been recaptured near Parkhurst Prison.*

a  Famous film star leaves $3,000,000 to her favourite pet
b  Priceless painting stolen from Louvre
c  Seven people killed in train crash
d  Princess runs away with gardener
e  President forced to resign
f  Sporting hero fails drug test

2  Choose two of the headlines and write the full stories. Read your news to the rest of the class.

3  What's in the news today? What national or international stories do you know?

### 2 Giving personal news

What about your personal news? What have you done today? This week? This year? Ask and answer questions with a partner.

Example
have/breakfast?

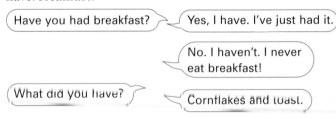

Have you had breakfast? — Yes, I have. I've just had it.

No. I haven't. I never eat breakfast!

What did you have? — Cornflakes and toast.

| Today | This week | This year |
|---|---|---|
| travel/by bus? | go/cinema? (Careful!) | have/a holiday yet? |
| do/any work? | do/any exercise? | move/house? |
| have/a coffee break? | play/a sport? | have/your birthday yet? |
| have/lunch yet? | watch/TV? | take/any exams? |
| do/any exercise? | wash/your hair? | apply/for a new job? |

## 3 Discussing grammar

Work in pairs.

1 Read the following sentences. Discuss where the words can go. Sometimes there are several possibilities.

| just | yet | already | ever | never |
| --- | --- | --- | --- | --- |

a I've washed my hair.
b Have you played basketball?
c He hasn't learned to drive.
d They've finished the exercise.
e She's learned a foreign language.
f We've met your teacher.
g Have they finished doing the washing-up?
h Has it stopped raining?

2 <u>Underline</u> the correct verb form.

a The Prime Minister of Italy *has resigned/has been resigned* and a new prime minister *has elected/has been elected*.
b The Italian people *told/were told* of his resignation on television yesterday evening.
c I *lost/have lost* my glasses. *Did you see/Have you seen* them anywhere?
d 'Where *has* Liz *gone/did* Liz *go* on holiday?' 'She's in Paris.'
e 'Where *has* Liz *gone/did* Liz *go* on holiday?' 'She went to Paris.'
f '*Did* John ever *go/Has* John ever *been* to Paris?' 'Oh, yes. Five times.'
g A huge earthquake *has hit/has been hit* central Japan. Nearly 1,000 people *have killed/have been killed*. It *happened/has happened* mid-afternoon yesterday.

## LANGUAGE REVIEW

### The Present Perfect

The Present Perfect relates past time to present time. It has three main uses.

1 To express unfinished past.

*I've lived here for five years.* (I started living here five years ago and I still live here.)
*He's been a teacher since he was twenty-one.*
NOT * He is a teacher since …

2 To express an experience that happened some time in your life. It is the experience that is important, not when it happened.

*I've been to Australia. I went three years ago.*
'*Have you ever lived in France?*' '*Yes, I have. I lived there from 1993 to 1995.*'

3 To express the present importance of a past event, usually a recent event. It is often used when giving news.

*The police have warned the public that the man is dangerous.*
*I've lost my credit card. Have you seen it?*

### The Present Perfect passive

The uses of the Present Perfect are the same in the passive.

*Two million cars have been produced so far this year.* (Unfinished past)
'*Have you ever been made redundant?*' '*No, never, thank goodness!*' (Past experience)
'*Have you heard? I've been left £4,000 by my great aunt!*' (Present importance)

Grammar Reference: page 135.

## READING AND SPEAKING

### Pre-reading task

1 Close your eyes for a few minutes. Imagine it is one hundred years ago and you are very rich.

– What is your life like?
– Where do you live? What do you do?
– Do you have any servants? How many? What do they do for you?
– What do you know about the lives of your servants? Where do they live?

2 Work in small groups and discuss your ideas in your group. Share your ideas with the rest of the class.

3 What about now? Do many people have servants?

Have you ever worked in anyone else's home? In what ways are servants today different from years ago?

## Reading

# The modern servant –
the nanny, the cook, and the gardener

1 You are going to read about three modern servants. Divide into three groups.

**Group A**  Read about the nanny.
**Group B**  Read about the cook.
**Group C**  Read about the gardener.

Read your article and answer the questions. Use your dictionary to help with new words. Discuss your answers with your group.

a What and who influenced her/his choice of career?
b What did her/his parents want her/him to do?
c What was the parents' attitude to the choice of career at first?
d Has the parents' attitude changed? If so, why?
e In what ways do the parents think that times have changed since they were young?

2 Read your article again.
Which of the following multi-word verbs can you find in your article? Underline them.

| | |
|---|---|
| bring up (1) | look after, educate (a child) |
| bring up (2) | mention (in conversation) |
| carry on | continue |
| drop out | leave, not complete (a college course) |
| fall out | quarrel and no longer be friends |
| get on with | have a good relationship with |
| get over | recover from (an illness, a shock) |
| give up | stop (a job, a habit, e.g. smoking) |
| go through | experience |
| grow up | change from child to adult |
| look after | take care of |
| make up (1) | invent |
| make it up (2) | be friends again after an argument |
| pick up | learn unconsciously (e.g. a language) |
| put off | postpone |
| be taken aback | be surprised |
| take after | resemble |
| turn out | be in the end |
| take over | take control of |

# The nanny

**A**manda Peniston-Bird, 21, is the daughter of a judge and has just completed a two-year training course to be a nanny at the Norland Nursery Training College. She and her mother talk about her choice of career.

## Amanda

My sister Charlotte was born when I was seven and my mother decided she needed a nanny to look after us. So we got Alison. She was very young, seventeen I think, and wonderful. I adored her. She only worked part-time with us before she started her training at Norland College. She had to dress us in the morning and take me to school. After school she made us delicious teas and read us stories in bed. On Charlotte's birthday she organized a fantastic party.

When Alison left, we had a trained nanny who lived with us and worked full-time. She was called Nanny Barnes by everyone, including my parents. She was older and quite traditional and wore a uniform. It was then that I realized that I wanted to be a nanny. I have always got on well with

'My father wanted me to be a solicitor.'

children. I have always enjoyed taking care of my sister and younger cousins. I told Mummy very firmly that I wanted to be a nanny when I grew up. At the time she laughed. I know that she and Daddy

thought it was just a childish phase I was going through, but it wasn't. They thought I would follow in my father's footsteps and study law. But I didn't. There were some terrible rows but I didn't go to university. I left school and spent a year working at Ludgrove School, where Prince William used to go. Then I started my training course at Norland College. I finished the course last month and I've applied for the post of nanny to twins aged six months. Mummy and Daddy weren't angry for long, we made it up before I went to college, and they have encouraged me ever since.

## Amanda's mother

*Her father is still a wee bit disappointed that she didn't take after him and study law, but I think we're both proud, and also pleased, that she has made her own decisions in life and done so well. We have brought her up to be an independent thinker, so we can't complain. Everything has turned out for the best. I had a nanny when I was a child but I never thought of being one myself, but times have changed and 'nannying' has been socially acceptable for a long time. It wasn't just Princess Diana who made it fashionable!*

# The cook

Giles Mildmay, 24, has been a professional cook for three years. His father, George, owns a two-hundred acre farm in Devon. The family have farmed in Devon for over three hundred years. Giles' younger brother Tobias is studying farm management at Exeter University. Giles and his father talk about his choice of career.

## Giles

I think I've always been interested in food. My grandparents (on my mother's side) lived in a huge old manor house in Lincolnshire and they had a wonderful cook. She made fantastic standard English food; her roast beef and Yorkshire pudding was out of this world. I used to love going down to the kitchen and watching her work, and I picked up a lot of cooking tips from her. I realized that I wanted to be a cook when I was about 12. I went to a boarding school and when other boys chose to do sport, I chose cookery. By the time I was

### 'My grandfather thinks I'm mad!'

15, I had taken over the cooking at home for my parents' dinner parties, and I had started to make up my own recipes. I knew my parents would not approve of cooking as a career, so I decided to introduce them slowly to the idea. I told them that I wanted to do a cookery course for fun, and I went for a month to a hotel in Torquay. I enjoyed it so much, I knew I couldn't put off telling my parents any longer, so I brought the subject up one night over dinner. At first there was silence, and then my father asked me why. I explained that cooking was like painting a picture or writing a book. Every meal was an act of creation. I could see that my father was not convinced, but he didn't get angry, he just patted me on the shoulder and smiled. My mother kissed me. And now that I have opened my own restaurant, I think they are very proud of me. However, my grandfather (on my father's side) is not so kind, he thinks I'm mad to have given up farming.

## Giles' father

*I know that times have changed, but I was brought up with a butler and a cook to look after me, and I never went near the kitchen. I was taken aback at first when Giles announced what he wanted to do. His grandfather still hasn't got over it, but his mother and I are delighted that he is doing something he enjoys. Nowadays anyone with a job that they enjoy is very lucky.*

# The gardener

Hugo Grantchester, 26, has been a gardener and a tree surgeon for four years. He went to Oxford University to study archaeology, but he dropped out after just one term. His father, Hector, is a surveyor and his mother, Geraldine, is an interior designer. Hugo and his mother talk about his choice of career.

## Hugo

When I was 11, we moved to a large Tudor house in East Anglia which had three acres of garden. We had a gardener who lived in a little cottage at the end of our drive. I used to spend hours watching him work and talking to him. I think I picked up a lot about gardening without realizing it, because one summer, when I was still at school, I took a job at a garden centre and I knew all the names of the plants, and I could give people advice. Then I went to university and it was a disaster. After a term I told my parents that I was going to give it up and go back to work in the garden centre. They were furious, we had a terrible row, and they didn't speak to me for months. But I knew it was a waste of time to carry on studying archaeology, and the moment I started gardening again, I knew I'd made the right decision. I've enjoyed every moment of the last four years and my parents have learnt to accept what I do, not only because they can see how happy I am, but also because a lot of my university friends have found it difficult to find good jobs or have been made redundant. Sometimes people are quite taken aback when they find out that their gardener went to university, but I think it makes them respect my opinion more when I'm helping them plan their gardens.

## Hugo's mother

*His father and I were so delighted when he went to Oxford, but when he gave it up so soon we were very, very angry. We thought manual labour was not the career for our only son. We fell out for months, Hector refused to allow Hugo into the house, and we all felt thoroughly miserable. But our daughter told us not to worry because Hugo would be a millionaire by the time he was forty. Anyway, we've made it up now we can see how happy he is, even though he hasn't become a millionaire yet! Times have changed and all kinds of people do all kinds of work, and I think the world's a better place for it!*

### 'My parents were furious.'

## Comprehension check

Find a partner from each of the other two groups.

1 Go through questions a–e in Exercise 1 on page 70 together. Compare and swap information about the people.

2 Read the other two articles quickly. Are the following statements true (✓) or false (✗)?

a Only Giles and Hugo were influenced by the servants in their families when they were children.
b Amanda wanted to be a nanny because she liked the uniform.
c Giles wanted to be a cook because the meals were so bad at boarding school.
d Hugo did well in his holiday job because he had learnt a lot about plants from the gardener.
e All of the parents were very angry when they were told about the choice of career.
f Hugo's parents were the least angry.
g All of the parents have become friends with their children again.
h Giles' grandfather has not forgiven him for becoming a cook.
i Some of the children have regretted their decision not to go to university.
j Hugo has already become a millionaire.

3 Show each other which multi-word verbs appear in your article. Discuss their meaning.
Which ones appear in more than one article?

## Roleplay

Work in groups of three.

### Students A and B

You are the parents of **C**. One of you is a doctor and the other a lawyer, and you would like **C** to follow one of these professions, but **C** has other ideas. Explain to **C** why yours are such good careers.

### Student C

**A** and **B** are your parents. They want you to become a lawyer or a doctor, but you have different ideas! You want to be one of the following (or choose one of your own):

a dancer   a musician   a poet   an explorer
a model   a jockey   an astronaut   ...

Talk together, and try to persuade each other to see your point of view.

## ● VOCABULARY

### Multi-word verbs

There are many examples of multi-word verbs in the reading texts.

*She needed a nanny to **look after** us.*
*I told my parents that I was going to **give** it **up**.*
*I wanted to be a nanny when I **grew up**.*

📖 Grammar Reference: page 136.

Use your dictionary to do these exercises.

**1 Meaning**

In the following groups of sentences *one* meaning of the multi-word verb is literal and *two* are idiomatic. Say which is which.

1 a The plane to Hong Kong has just *taken off*.
   b *Take* that vase *off* the table. It's going to fall.
   c He's very famous now. His popularity really *took off* when he made that film.

2 a I'll *bring* you *up* some water when I come to bed.
   b Have you *brought up* the question of borrowing the money?
   c They *brought up* six children with very little money.

3 a Her health has really *picked up* since she moved to a sunny climate.
   b Can you *pick up* my pen for me? It's under your chair.
   c I *picked up* a little Italian when I was working in Rome.

Buongiorno! Come ti chiami?

4 a It took me a long time to *get over* the operation.
   b Mario doesn't speak much English so it was difficult to *get over* to him what I wanted.
   c Can you help me *get over* this wall? The gate is closed.

5 a I *looked up* Bob's number in the phone book.
   b The new manager is very good. Sales have really *looked up* since he came.
   c We *looked up* the tree and there was the cat on the top branch.

## 2 Verbs with two particles

Complete the pairs of sentences with one of the following multi-word verbs.

put up with    go out with    get on with    run out of    look forward to

a I don't _____ my sister's husband very well.
  Our teacher told us to _____ our work quietly.

b Has the photocopier _____ paper again?
  The children always _____ school immediately the bell goes.

c Why don't you ever _____ Christmas?
  We always _____ going on holiday.

d I must _____ the dog. She hasn't been for a walk yet.
  Tom and Flora used to _____ each other when they were teenagers.

e How do you manage to _____ the noise from your neighbours?
  Some parents _____ a lot of bad behaviour from their kids.

In which pairs of sentences is the meaning the same? In which is the meaning different?

## 3 Separable or inseparable?

Check whether the multi-word verb in the following sentences is separable or not.
Replace the word in *italics* with the pronoun.

**Example**
He turned on *the light*.    *He turned **it** on.*
She takes after *her father*.    *She takes after **him**.*

a I've just looked up *the word* in my dictionary.
b He's looking after *my cats* while I'm away.
c She has brought up *those children* really well.
d We picked up *Spanish* very quickly.
e I don't think they'll ever get over *the shock of her death*.
f He's taken up *golf* because he has a lot of free time since he retired.

## ● LISTENING AND SPEAKING

### Pre-listening task

Work in groups and discuss the following questions.

– Is anyone in your family retired? Who?
– What job did they do before retiring?
– How old were they when they retired?
– How long have they been retired?
– What do they do now?

### Listening

Look at the photograph of Thomas Wilson and his granddaughter, Philippa. Thomas used to be the managing director of a large textile company. He has now retired.

**T.51** Listen to him talking to Philippa. Who do you think is happier, Thomas or Philippa? Why?

### Comprehension check

1 Underline the correct question form and then answer it.

a How long *was he/has he been* retired?
b How long *did he work/has he worked* for the textile company?
c How long *was he/has he been* married?
d Who *did he go/has he gone* to Wales with?

2 Why does he like playing golf?
3 Which countries has he visited since he retired? Where did he go two years ago?
4 Why is he brown?
5 Who are the following: Rover, Keith, Miriam, Kylie, and Helen?
6 What are the two sad events in Thomas' life?
7 What does Philippa complain about?
8 What does Thomas mean when he says, 'You only get one go at it!'?

*Thomas Wilson*
*– a retired man –*

## Discussion

- What is the usual retirement age for men and women in your country?
- What kind of thing do people like doing when they retire?
- Are attitudes to retirement changing?
- What do you think is the best age to retire?
- When would you like to retire?
- What would you like to do when you retire?

## ● WRITING

### Formal letters

1   Read Nancy's letter of application to *Worldwatch*. Put *one* word into each gap.

Compare your answers with a partner.

2   Look at Nancy's letter again.

- In what other ways can you begin and end formal letters?
- In what ways can you begin and end informal letters?
- Where is Nancy's address written?
- Where is the address of the company she's writing to?
- In what other way can you write the date?
- Where does Nancy sign her name? Where does she print her name?

There are three paragraphs. What is the aim of each one?

3   Write a letter of application for the following job in the *Daily News*.

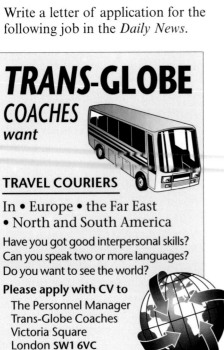
17 Hillside Rd
Chesswood
Herts. WD3 5LB
Tel 01923 284171
Fax 01923 286622

Thursday 17 January

David Benton
Worldwatch UK Ltd
357 Ferry Rd
Basingstoke RG2 5HP

Dear Mr Benton

I saw your _____ for a Business Journalist in today's Guardian newspaper. I am very _____ in the job and I think that I have many of the necessary _____ .

I _____ politics and modern languages at Oxford University. I am _____ in French, German and Spanish. I have _____ widely in Europe and South America, and I _____ worked as a business journalist for the BBC _____ the last five years.

I enclose a copy of my curriculum vitae. I look forward _____ hearing from you soon. Please let me know if you need more information.

Yours sincerely

*Nancy Mann*

Nancy Mann

## On the telephone

1 All the phrases below are from typical telephone calls. Match a line in **A** with a line in **B**.

**A**

a Hello, this is Chesswood 285120. I'm afraid I'm not at home at the moment, but please leave your name and number after the tone and I'll get back to you as soon as I can.

b I'm afraid Mr Barrett's in a meeting. Can I take a message?

c Shall I ask Miss Jackson to give you a call when she gets back?

d Good morning. Payne and Stracey Advertising.

e Hello, Mrs Barrett … I'm afraid Mr Barrett's on another line at the moment. Do you want to hold or …? Oh, he's free now. I'm putting you through.

f Hello. Is that Sandra?

**B**

☐ Good morning. Can I have extension 321, please?

☐ No, I'm sorry, it isn't. She's just gone out. Can I take a message? She'll be back in a minute.

☐ Hi, Annie. This is er … Pete here. Pete Nealy. Er … I need to speak to you about next weekend. Can you give me a ring? Erm … I'm at home, by the way. It's ten o'clock now and I'll be here all morning, er … until two o'clock. Yes, thanks. Bye.

☐ Thank you very much. Frank? It's me, Diana.

☐ Yes, please. This is Pam Haddon. He rang me earlier and left a message on my answer phone and I'm returning his call. Can you tell him I'm back in my office now?

☐ Yes, please. I'm sure she's got my number but I'll give it to you again, just in case. It's 01924 561718.

2 **T.52** Listen and check your answers. Which sound more like business calls?

3 Notice these common expressions on the telephone.

a A Hello!
  B Hello. Could I speak to Barry Perkins, please?
  A Speaking. (= I am Barry Perkins.)
  B Ah, hello. This is Jane Gardener. (NOT *I'm … or * Here is …)

b A Can I have extension 366, please?
  B Hold the line, please. I'm putting you through.

c A Can I speak to Mrs Barrett, please?
  B I'm afraid she's out at the moment. Can I take a message?
  A Yes. Can you ask her to give me a ring? I'll give you my number.

d A Can I speak to Mr Bray, please?
  B I'm afraid his line is busy at the moment. Would you like to hold?
  A No. I'll phone back later.

## Leaving a message on an answer phone

1 It can be difficult to leave a message on an answer phone! You have to think quickly and speak clearly, and you have to pretend that you're talking to a person, but of course you're talking to a machine!

*Help! Help! Help!*

# HOW to leave a message on an answer phone!

| introduce yourself ▶▶▶ | Hello. This is … My name is … |
| give the day and time ▶▶ | It's three o'clock on Monday afternoon. |
| reason for phoning ▶▶▶ | I'm ringing … to let you know that … to find out if … because I need … |
| request action ▶▶▶▶▶▶ | Could you ring me back? help me? |
| give your number ▶▶▶▶▶ | My number is … You can get me on … I'm on 784 567 until five o'clock. |
| end ▶▶▶▶▶▶▶▶▶▶▶▶ | Thanks a lot. Goodbye. |

2 Work in pairs.
Your teacher will give you role cards. Act out a telephone conversation!

# Imagine!

Conditionals
Time clauses
*would*
Making suggestions

---

## 8

**1** Look at the pictures. Put the words under each picture in the right order to complete the sentences.

a I usually get the bus to school, but ...

get I if up late lift me Dad gives a my

if _____

b I've got my driving test next week, and ...

pass I test the if buy I'll car a new

if _____

c I don't have any money at all, but ...

million won I a if
round I'd the pounds
travel world

if _____

_____

**2** Which situation ... is always true?
... expresses a future possibility?
... is possible but improbable?

## PRESENTATION (1)

### First conditional and time clauses

1 **T.53a** Jim is going to fly to Istanbul, and then he's going to backpack around the world with his friend, Anthony. His mother is very worried! Listen to their conversation. Put the words from the box in the gaps.

| will you do | won't get | 'll be | 'll get |
|---|---|---|---|
| 'll ask | won't do | get | 'll be |

**Mum** Oh, dear! I hope everything will be all right. You've never been abroad before.

**Jim** Don't worry, Mum. I _____ OK. I can look after myself. Anyway, I _____ with Anthony. We _____ anything stupid.

**Mum** But what _____ if you run out of money?

**Jim** We _____ a job of course!

**Mum** Oh. What about if you get lost?

**Jim** Mum! If we _____ lost, we _____ someone the way, but we _____ lost because we know where we're going!

**Mum** Oh. All right. But what if ...?

Practise the dialogue in pairs.

2 Make similar dialogues about other things that Jim's mother is worried about. Use *you* and *I*.

> Oh dear! What will you do if you get food poisoning?

> Don't worry, Mum. I'll …

– get food poisoning
– lose your passport
– meet a girl who you fall in love with
– get sunburnt
– are homesick
– are mugged

– don't like the food
– don't understand the language
– don't get on with Anthony

3  **T.53b**  Listen to the next part of their conversation. Put the verb into the correct tense.

Mum   But how will I know that you're all right?
Jim    When we _____ (get) to a big city, I _____ (send) you a postcard.
Mum   Oh. But Jim, it's such a long flight to Istanbul!
Jim    Mum! As soon as we _____ (arrive) in Turkey, I _____ (give) you a ring!
Mum   I _____ (be) so worried until I _____ (hear) from you.
Jim    It'll be OK, Mum. Honest!

● Grammar questions

– Which sentence expresses a future possibility, and which a future certainty?

  *If we run out of money, we'll get a job.*
  *When we get to a big city, I'll send you a postcard.*

– Tick (✓) the one that is right. Cross out (✗) the one that is wrong.

  ☐ *If we get lost, …*
  ☐ *If we'll get lost, …*

  ☐ *When we go …*
  ☐ *When we'll go …*

  ☐ *As soon as we arrive, …*
  ☐ *As soon as we'll arrive, …*

# PRACTICE

## 1 Completing a conversation

1 Joe (**J**) is saying goodbye to his wife, Sue (**S**), who is going for a job interview. Put *if*, *when*, or *as soon as* into each box. Put the verb into the correct tense.

J   Goodbye, darling! Good luck with the interview!

S   Thanks. I'll need it. I hope the trains are running on time. [____] the trains _____ (be) delayed, I _____ (get) a taxi. [____] I _____ (be) late for the interview, I _____ (be) furious with myself!

J   Just keep calm! Phone me when you can.

S   I will. [____] I _____ (come) out of the interview, I _____ (give) you a ring.

J   When _____ you _____ (know) [____] you've got the job?

S   They _____ (send) me a letter in the next few days. [____] they _____ (offer) me the job, I _____ (accept) it, and [____] I accept it, we _____ (have to) move house. You know that, don't you?

J   Sure. But we'll worry about that later.

S   OK. What are you doing today?

J   I can't remember. [____] I _____ (get) to the office, I _____ (look) in my diary. I don't think I'm doing much today.

S   Don't forget to pick up the children [____] you _____ (get) back from work.

J   I won't. You'd better go now. [____] you _____ (not hurry), you _____ (miss) the train.

S   OK. I _____ (see) you this evening. Bye!

J   Bye, my love. Take care, and good luck!

  **T.54**   Listen and check your answers.

2 In pairs, ask and answer questions about Joe and Sue's conversation.

  Example
  What/Sue/do/if/trains/delayed?
  *What will Sue do if the trains are delayed?*
  *She'll get a taxi.*

a   How/she/feel/if/late for the interview?
b   When/Sue/phone/Joe?
c   When/know/if/she's got the job?
d   What/she/do/if/they/offer her the job?
e   What/they/have to do/if/she/accept/job?
f   What/Joe/do/when/get/office?
g   What/happen/if/Sue/not hurry?

# PRESENTATION (2)

## Second conditional and *would*

1  Is there a national lottery in your country?
How much can you win?
In Britain you can win more than £10 million a week!

**T.55**  Look at the pictures and listen to some people
saying what they would do if they won £2 million.
Try to guess who says what and write a number in the
box. Write notes on what they would do with it.
Practise some of the sentences.

2  Complete these sentences from the interviews.

a  'I _____ on a boat trip around the world.'
'Oh, I _____ . I _____ so bored.
I _____ fly. It _____ so much
quicker!'

b  'I _____ taking things easy for a bit, but
then I _____ to just get on with my life, 'cos
I'm very happy, really, with what I've got.'

Practise some of the sentences with *would*.
Notice the contraction *it'd* /ɪtəd/.

## ● Grammar questions

–  Read the example below. Do we use the past tense
forms *had* and *would* to refer to past time, or to show
unreality?

*If I had £2 million, I would go round the world.*

–  *I'd rather* (= I would rather) + infinitive means the
same as *I'd prefer to* …

*I don't like studying. I'd rather be outside playing
tennis.*

–  *I wouldn't mind* + noun or *-ing* means *I would (quite)
like* …

*I wouldn't mind a cup of tea.*
*I wouldn't mind having a few weeks off work.*

## PRACTICE

### 1 Discussion

What would *you* do with two million pounds?
Work in groups. Ask and answer questions.

a  What … buy?
b  How much … give away? Who … give it to?
c  … go on holiday? Where … to?
d  What about your job? … carry on working or … give
up your job?
e  … go on a spending spree?
f  How much … invest?
g  … be happier than you are now?

## 2 Various conditional forms

1 Match a line in **A** with a line in **B** and a line in **C**.

| | A | B | C |
|---|---|---|---|
| a | If Tony rings, | don't wait for me. | It would be really useful for work. |
| b | If you've finished your work, | I might do an evening class. | He can get hold of me there. |
| c | If I'm not back by 8.00, | you have to have a visa. | Keep warm and have plenty of fluids. |
| d | If you've got the 'flu, | you must give me a ring. | But you must be back here in fifteen minutes. |
| e | If you're ever in London, | tell him I'm at Andy's. | We could go out somewhere. |
| f | If you go to Australia, | you can have a break. | I'd love to be really good at photography. |
| g | I'd buy a word processor | you should go to bed. | You can get one from the Embassy. |
| h | If I had more time, | if I could afford it. | Go without me. I'll join you at the party. |

**T.56a** Listen and check your answers. Practise some of the sentences. Look at the lines in **A** and **B**. What are the different possible verb forms?

> Notice that when we have a conditional sentence with two present tenses, it expresses a situation that is always true. *If* means *when* or *whenever*. This is called the **zero conditional**.
>
> *If you boil water, it evaporates.*

2 **T.56b** You will hear some questions. Say if they are examples of the first, second or zero conditional. In pairs, practise the questions and answer them.

## 3 Dialogues with *will* and *would*

Work in pairs.
Look at the following situations. Decide if they are …
… possible;
… imaginary and probably won't happen.

Ask and answer questions about what you *will do* or *would do* in each situation.

**Example**
There's a good film on TV tonight. (*Possible*)
*What will you do if there's a good film on TV tonight?*
*I'll watch it.*

You find burglars in your flat. (*Imaginary*)
*What would you do if you found burglars in your flat?*
*I'd phone the police.*

a You can't do this exercise.
b The weather's good this weekend.
c A good friend invites you out tonight.
d You are the president of your country.
e You don't have any homework tonight.
f Your teacher gives you extra homework tonight.
g You can speak perfect English.

## LANGUAGE REVIEW

### First conditional

First conditional sentences express real possibilities. Notice that we do not usually use *will* in the *if* clause.

*If I see a nice jumper in the shops, I'll buy it.*
*What will you do if you don't have enough money?*

### Second conditional

Second conditional sentences express unreal or improbable situations. We use past tense forms to show 'unreality' and distance from the present.

*What would you do if you saw a ghost?*
*If I were Prime Minister, I'd increase income tax.*

Both first and second conditional sentences refer to the present and future. The difference is not about time but probability.

*If I win the tennis match, I'll …* (I think it's possible)
*If I won £5 million, I'd …* (but I don't think it'll happen)

### Zero conditional

Zero conditional sentences refer to 'all time', not just the present or future. They express a situation that is always true. *If* means *when* or *whenever*.

*If I read too much, I get a headache.*
*If you drop an egg, it breaks.*

### Time clauses

We do not usually use *will* in time clauses.

*I'll give you a ring* | *before I go.*
| *as soon as I get back.*
| *when I know the time of the train.*

📖 Grammar Reference: page 137.

## ● READING AND A SONG

### Pre-reading task

1 Look at the title of the magazine article. It is based on a well-known song from a 1950s' American musical.

   **T.57** Listen to one or two verses of the song. What *don't* the singers of the song want to do? What *do* they want to do? The tapescript is on page 127.

2 The article is about people who win huge amounts of money in a lottery or on the football pools, and how this affects their lives. Which of the following do you think are good suggestions (✓) or bad suggestions (✗) for such people?

   If you win a lot of money, …

   … you should give up work. ☐
   … you should buy a new house. ☐
   . . . you mustn't let it change you. ☐
   … it's a good idea to keep it a secret. ☐
   … you should give money to everyone who asks for it. ☐
   … you should go on a spending spree. ☐

   What suggestions would *you* give to someone who has won a lot of money?

3 The words in **A** are in the article. Match a word in **A** with a definition in **B**.

| A | B |
|---|---|
| envy | a sum of money you receive unexpectedly |
| to fantasize | an aim, a reason for doing something |
| a jigsaw | a feeling of discontent because someone has something that you want |
| a windfall | to spend money foolishly on small, useless things |
| a purpose | to imagine, to dream |
| to fritter away money | a picture cut into pieces that you have to put together again |

### Reading

Read the article. The following sentences have been taken out of the text. Where do you think they should go?

a They were furious!
b we feel at home
c It is tempting to move to a bigger house
d 'nothing but misery'
e what the money would do to us!
f it seems fantastic!
g most of their money will be frittered away
h if you lent him some money,

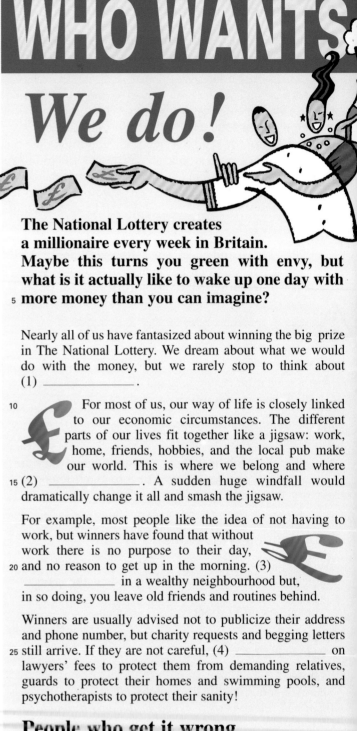

# WHO WANTS
## *We do!*

**The National Lottery creates a millionaire every week in Britain. Maybe this turns you green with envy, but what is it actually like to wake up one day with**
5 **more money than you can imagine?**

Nearly all of us have fantasized about winning the big prize in The National Lottery. We dream about what we would do with the money, but we rarely stop to think about (1) _____ .

10 For most of us, our way of life is closely linked to our economic circumstances. The different parts of our lives fit together like a jigsaw: work, home, friends, hobbies, and the local pub make our world. This is where we belong and where
15 (2) _____ . A sudden huge windfall would dramatically change it all and smash the jigsaw.

For example, most people like the idea of not having to work, but winners have found that without work there is no purpose to their day,
20 and no reason to get up in the morning. (3) _____ in a wealthy neighbourhood but, in so doing, you leave old friends and routines behind.

Winners are usually advised not to publicize their address and phone number, but charity requests and begging letters
25 still arrive. If they are not careful, (4) _____ on lawyers' fees to protect them from demanding relatives, guards to protect their homes and swimming pools, and psychotherapists to protect their sanity!

## People who get it wrong

30 There are many stories about people who can't learn how to be rich. In 1989, Val Johnson won £850,000 on the pools. Immediately, she went on a spending spree that lasted for four years and five marriages. She is now penniless and alone. 'I'm not a happy person,' she says.
35 'Winning money was the most awful thing that happened to me.'

Then there is the story of Alice Hopper, who says that her £950,000 win four years ago brought her (5) _____ . She walked out of the factory where
40 she worked, and left a goodbye note for her husband on the

# TO BE A MILLIONAIRE?

kitchen table. She bought herself a villa in Spain, and two bars (one a birthday present for her eighteen-year-old son). After three months, her son was killed while driving home from the bar on the motorbike which his mother had also
45 bought for him. She found the bars more and more difficult to run. She now sings in a local Karaoke bar to earn money for groceries. 'I wish I was still working in the factory,' she says.

## 'It won't change us!'

That's what all winners say when they talk to reporters and
50 television cameras as they accept the cheque and the kisses from a famous film star. And some winners, like Malcolm Price, really mean it. He refused to change his way of life when he won £2.5 million. The next Saturday night, he went to his local pub as
55 usual, and as usual he *didn't* buy his friends a drink. (6) _____ . He, too, is a lonely man now.

Imagine you are an average family and you have just won £1 million. At first (7) _____ . Just by picking up the phone you can get the toilet seat fixed, and the leak in
60 the roof repaired — all the problems that have been making your life miserable. 'But, it won't change us, darling,' you say to your wife. 'Yes, it will!' she insists. 'I want it to change us. It will make life better! It'll be brilliant!'

Already the children are changing. Just this morning they
65 were ordinary, contented kids. Now they are demanding computer games, CD players, motorbikes … 'Hold on!' you shout. 'Let me answer the door.'

It is your neighbour, with a bunch of flowers and a loving smile on her face. 'Congratulations!' she shouts. 'I was
70 wondering if you could lend me …' You shut the door.

In the first week you receive two thousand letters advising you how to spend your money, either by investing it or giving it to good causes. Your son comes home with a music system that is bigger than the
75 living-room, your sixteen-year-old daughter books a holiday to Barbados with her boyfriend, and your wife buys a Rolls-Royce. 'But darling,' you say, 'we haven't received one penny of this money yet! What about the broken toilet seat? What
80 about the leaking roof? What about me?' 'I haven't forgotten you,' says your wife. 'I've bought you a racehorse!'

The next day you get a begging letter from a man who won the lottery a year ago. He tells you how he spent £2,000,000
85 in three weeks. He says (8) _____ , he could start his life all over again. You begin to think that winning a fortune brings more problems than it solves! You realize that you are quite fond of the broken toilet seat and the leaking roof after all.

◄ **Paul Maddison and Mark Gardiner celebrate with their wives**

▼ **David Caldwell splashes out with Joanna Lumley**

## £ A final thought

90 When you next buy your lottery ticket, or do the football pools, just stop for a minute and ask yourself why you're doing it. Do you actually want to win? Or are you doing it for the excitement of thinking about winning?

## Comprehension check

1 Look back at the suggestions in the Pre-reading task. Have you changed your mind about any of them?

2 Answer the questions.
a Does the magazine article talk more about the positive side of winning a lot of money, or the negative side?
b How can a large amount of money affect …
… our work?    … our home?    … our friends?
c How does the article say money can be 'frittered away'?
d The following groups are mentioned in the article: charities, relatives, lawyers, security guards, psychotherapists.
Which of them is speaking in the following lines?

'Tell me about your relationship with your father.'
'Twenty pounds will feed a family for a month. Please give generously.'
'Now, John, you know you've always been my favourite nephew.'
'Sorry, sir. You can't go any further without permission.'
'I strongly advise you to take them to court.'

e Give three facts each about the lives of Val Johnson, Alice Hopper, and Malcolm Price.
Why are they all mentioned?
f In the imaginary family that has won £1 million, who says, 'It won't change us'? Who says, 'I want it to change us'?
g What do the children want to have? What does the neighbour want?
h Who in the family doesn't buy anything? What do the others buy?

## What do you think?

1  In what way is our life like a jigsaw?
2  How does winning a large amount of money smash the jigsaw?
3  Why do we need work in our lives?
4  In the story of the family that has won £1 million, what is the joke about the toilet seat?
5  What does he mean when he says, 'It won't change us'? What does his wife want to change?
6  What for you are the answers to the questions in the last paragraph of 'Who wants to be a millionaire?'?

## Vocabulary

Find a word or words in the text that mean the same as the following definitions. They are in the same order as they appear in the text.

a  not often
b  very big
c  break violently
d  area around your house
e  asking (for something) very strongly
f  keep (something) safe, defend
g  a time when you go to the shops and spend a lot of money
h  having not a penny
i  basic things to eat like bread, sugar, vegetables
j  a hole through which water gets in

## ● SPEAKING

### A maze

Work in groups and read the role card below.

Congratulations! Or is it? You have won five million pounds. What are you going to do with it? Talk together until you all agree on what to do next. Your teacher will then give you a card with more information, and another decision to make.

Carry on talking until you come to the end. The aim is to spend your money wisely without going mad!

*Congratulations!*
You have won
**£5 MILLION!**
~
***Now* you have to make some decisions.**
**Are you going to keep your win a secret,
or will you go to a big London hotel to receive
your cheque from a famous film star?
Of course the press will be there,
and your photo will be in all the newspapers.**

If you want to remain anonymous,
go to

If you want to go to the hotel and the press conference,
go to

## ● VOCABULARY

### Base and strong adjectives

1  Some adjectives have the idea of *very*. Look at these examples from the article on pages 80–81.

*a huge windfall*  —  *huge* means *very big*
*it seems fantastic*  —  *fantastic* means *very good*
*It'll be brilliant!*  —  *brilliant* means *very good*

2  Put a base adjective from the box next to a strong adjective.

| good | bad | cold | frightened |
|---|---|---|---|
| funny | tasty | angry | tired |
| pretty/attractive | interesting | | hot |
| surprised | clever | dirty | |

| Base adjective | Strong adjective |
|---|---|
| *big* | enormous, huge |
| _____ | boiling |
| _____ | exhausted |
| _____ | freezing |
| _____ | delicious |
| _____ | fascinating |
| _____ | horrid, horrible, awful, terrible, disgusting |
| _____ | perfect, marvellous, superb, wonderful, fantastic, brilliant |
| _____ | filthy |
| _____ | astonished, amazed |
| _____ | furious |
| _____ | hilarious |
| _____ | terrified |
| _____ | beautiful |
| _____ | brilliant |

We can make adjectives more extreme by using adverbs such as *very* and *absolutely*.
*Their house is very big.*
*But their garden is absolutely enormous.*

Careful! We cannot say *absolutely big because *absolutely* only goes with strong adjectives, and we cannot say *very enormous because *enormous* already means *very big*.

The following adverbs can be used:

| | |
|---|---|
| ***very* tired** | ***absolutely* exhausted** |
| ***quite* good** | ***absolutely* freezing** |
| ***really* cold** | ***really* wonderful** |

3 **T.58** Listen to the dialogues. Complete them, using an adverb and an adjective.

Example

> What did you do last night? — We went to the cinema.

> What did you see? — *Murder in the Park*.

> Was it good? — I thought it was *absolutely brilliant*, but Pete was *really terrified*. There was so much blood!

4 Make up similar dialogues. Talk about: a person, a meal, the weather, a book, an exam, the news.

## ● LISTENING

### Pre-listening task

1 Have you ever given money to charity, or worked for a charity?

2 Look at the list of charities and charitable causes below. Which do you think are the most and least deserving?

- a charity that helps old people with food and housing
- a hospice for people who are dying of an incurable disease
- an organization that encourages people to sponsor a child in the Third World
- a charity that helps homeless people in cities
- cancer research
- a charity that helps people with HIV or AIDS
- a group that believes we should not exploit animals in any way at all

### Listening

**T.59** Listen to three charity appeals and fill in the chart.

| | Who or what the charity tries to help | How the charity helps | Some of their successes and/or problems |
|---|---|---|---|
|  Amnesty International | | | |
|  Royal Society for the Prevention of Cruelty to Animals | | | |
| Drought and Famine in Africa | | | |

### What do you think?

Imagine that you have £5,000 that you want to give to charity.
Who would you give the money to? How would you divide it?
Think about what *you* would do, and then discuss your ideas with a partner.

# ● WRITING

## Words that join ideas

1 Some words and expressions are used to make a comment on what is being expressed.

Examples
'Ah, now, Peter! Come over here!'
'My name's Jack, **actually**.' (*Actually* = I'm going to give you some extra information that you didn't know, or that you got wrong.)

*What an awful journey you had! You must be exhausted!* **Anyway**, *you're here now so let's not worry any more.* (*Anyway* = let's change the subject and talk about something else.)

2 Some words are used to join ideas and sentences.

Example
George was rich. He wasn't a happy man.
*George was rich,* **but** *he wasn't a happy man.*
**Although** *George was rich, he wasn't a happy man.*
*George was rich.* **However**, *he wasn't a happy man.*

3 In the letter, choose the words that fit best. Nearly all the words have appeared in this unit. The letter is written by Jacky, who is married to Joe and has two children, Samantha and Polly.

---

### 16 Cassandra Gardens, London N16

*22 July*

*Dear Penny*

*I hope you're all well. We're all terribly busy,* (a) | even / for example | *Polly, who has finally managed to find some work.* (b) | Unfortunately, / Generally, | *it's not a very good job, but* (c) | therefore / at least | *it's a job, and maybe she will find something better in the future. She has* (d) | especially / also | *found somewhere else to live – a small flat about five miles away,* (e) | so / because | *now there's* (f) | nearly / only | *Joe and me left at home. After 24 years of having children to look after, it's very strange to have the house to ourselves,* (g) | although / so | *I do appreciate coming home to a tidy house at the end of a day. By the way, Polly has broken up with her boyfriend, Peter. We were very sorry,* (h) | because / but | *we got on well with him, and they seemed to be well-suited.*

*Samantha has some interesting news,* (i) | either. / as well. | *She passed her final exams. We heard last week, so* (j) | of course, / however, | *we had a small family celebration. She doesn't know what she wants to do yet,* (k) | so / but | *she has plenty of time to decide. She doesn't have a boyfriend at the moment,* (l) | either. / too. | *I don't know what's the matter with them! They're both* (m) | enough pretty! / pretty enough! | *Joe's fine, but he hasn't been able to do much in the garden* (n) | because / because of | *the weather, which has been terrible.* (o) | Actually / Meanwhile | *it has rained every day for the past fortnight. It's unbelievable, isn't it?*

(p) | After all, / Anyway, | *that's enough of my news. How are you all? What are you up to?*

*Do write soon and tell me everything!*

*Love*

*Jacky*

---

## Making suggestions

1 Maggie's bored and Paul's broke. Look at the suggestions made by their friends. Are they talking to Maggie or Paul? Which suggestions include the speaker?

> Let's go to the cinema!

> Why don't we go for a walk?

> If I were you, I'd get a better-paid job.

> I don't think you should go out so much.

> Why don't you ask your parents?

> Shall we have a game of cards?

> You ought to save some money every month!

> I'm broke!

> You'd better get a loan from the bank!

> I'm bored!

2 **T.60** Listen to Maggie and Paul and their friends. How can we make suggestions in English?

3 Listen again and read the tapescript on page 136. Notice how we accept and reject suggestions.

Work in pairs. Practise the dialogues. Take it in turns to cover the page.

4 Change the sentence using the prompts.

Example

Let's go to the cinema.

a Why don't we …?

> Why don't we go to the cinema?

b eat out tonight?

> Why don't we eat out tonight?

c I think we should

> I think we should eat out tonight.

| Let's go to the cinema. | Why don't you phone Pat? |
|---|---|
| a Why don't we …? | a You'd better |
| b eat out tonight? | b the police |
| c I think we should | c tell the truth |
| d invite Pete to dinner tomorrow | d If I were you, I'd |
| e redecorate the house | e look for a different job |
| f If I were you, I'd | f You should |
| g You ought to | g She |
| h buy some new clothes | h ought to |
| i go shopping | i have a break |
| j Shall we …? | j Let's |

5 Work in pairs. Make dialogues for the situations, using ways of making suggestions.

Example
You have got a terrible cold.

A *My head's killing me! And my nose is so sore!*
B *I think you should go to bed with a hot drink.*
A *That's a good idea. I'll go right now.*
B *I'll make you a hot lemon drink.*
A *Oh, that would be lovely!*

a You've just got a job in Moscow, so you need to learn the Russian language, and find out about Russian people and culture as quickly as possible.

b You both have the evening free, and there's nothing on TV.

c Your flat's a mess, it hasn't been decorated for ages, and the furniture is ancient. Suddenly you inherit some money!

d You can't decide whether to go to university (but you don't know what to study) or have a year off and go round the world.

e It's Christmas time! What can you buy for the teacher and the different members of the class?

f You've been invited to the Queen's garden party at Buckingham Palace in June. What are you going to wear? The weather in June is very unpredictable.

# 9 Relationships

## Modal verbs (2) probability
*So do I! Neither do I!*

---

### Test your grammar

1 Read the pairs of sentences. Which sentence in each pair expresses a fact? Put a ✓. Which sentence expresses a possibility? Put a ?.

Example
I'm in love!          ✓
I must be in love!   ?

a She's having a shower.
She could be having a shower.

b That pen's mine.
That pen might be mine.

c He doesn't own a Rolls Royce.
He can't own a Rolls Royce.

d You must have met my brother.
You've met my brother.

e They haven't met the Queen.
They can't have met the Queen.

f Shakespeare might have lived there.
Shakespeare lived there.

2 Which of the sentences in Exercise 1 are about the present? Which are about the past?

## PRESENTATION (1)

### Modal verbs of probability in the present

1 Do you ever read the Problem Page in magazines or newspapers? What kinds of problems do people often write about?

2 Here are the replies to letters from two people who wrote to Susie's Problem Page in *Metropolitan Magazine*. Read them and discuss with a partner what you think the problem is. Use your dictionary to check any new words.

# Susie's Problem page

**Lucy has a problem:**
"I live in Scotland and he lives in California! …"

*Dear Lucy*

Everyone has daydreams and there is nothing wrong with this. There is only a problem when you forget where dreams end and the real world begins. Don't write any more letters to him. It's a waste of time and money, and you know really that a relationship with him is impossible. For one thing he lives in California and you live in Scotland. Try to get out more and find some friends in the real world; sitting at home crying over his records won't help you. You need to find other interests and other people of your own age to talk to. Your parents clearly don't have enough time to listen. Study hard and good luck next June!

*Yours Susie*

3 Look at the texts. Say who *she*, *he*, or *they* refer to in the following sentences.

a She must be exhausted.

b She must be in love with a pop star.

c She could be a doctor or a nurse.

d She can't have many friends.

e He might be an alcoholic.

f He must be unemployed.

g They can't have a very good relationship with their daughter.

h They might not have any children.

i She can't get on very well with her daughter-in-law.

j She must be studying for exams next June.

k They might live near a busy road.

l He must snore.

4 Give reasons for each statement.

Example
*Pam must be exhausted … because she works hard, she does everything in the house and she can't sleep.*

**Pam has a problem:
"He spends all his time at his mother's! …"**

*Dear Pam*

If all you say is true, it is remarkable that you are still together. But you are not helping your relationship by saying nothing and doing everything. He doesn't seem to notice how you feel. I know he's worried about his mother but he seems to spend more time at her house than his own. You have a tiring and stressful job, caring for sick people all day, and it is unfair that he is always at his mother's and leaves you to do all the housework. The empty whisky bottles under the bed are also worrying. Perhaps he will feel better about himself when he finds work. In the meantime, you must try to talk openly to each other about your feelings, otherwise anger and resentment will grow. Also, buy some earplugs—you need a good night's sleep!

*Yours Susie*

● **Grammar questions**

– Which statement is the most sure? Which are less sure?

   She **must be** in love.
   She **could be** in love.
   She **might be** in love.

– The above sentences all express *I think it's probable/possible that she is in love.*
   How do you express *I don't think it's probable/possible that she is in love?*

## PRACTICE

## 1 Controlled speaking

Work in pairs.

**Student A**   Talk to Student B about Lucy.
**Student B**   Talk to Student A about Pam.

Put *one* suitable verb form into each gap.

**Student A**

Lucy _____ in Scotland so she must _____ Scottish. She _____ a lot of letters to a pop star in California, so she must _____ a lot of money on stamps. She _____ in her room and _____ to his music all of the time so she can't _____ many friends or hobbies. She should _____ out more and _____ some friends and then she might _____ the pop star. She could _____ to talk to her parents again, but they might not _____ because they _____ very busy.

**Student B**

Pam must _____ very tired at the end of the day because she _____ a stressful job. She must _____ sorry for her husband because he _____ unemployed but she must also _____ very angry with him because he never _____ any housework. She could _____ her mother-in-law to help but she can't _____ a very good relationship with her because her husband _____ too much time at her house. Things might _____ better if he could _____ a job and if they could _____ to each other.

## 2 Grammar and pronunciation

Respond to the statements or questions using the word or words in brackets.

Example
I haven't eaten anything since breakfast.
   (must, very)
*You must be very hungry!*

a  Mr and Mrs Brown never go on holiday.
   (can't, much money)
b  The phone's ringing! (might, Jane)
c  Paul's taking his umbrella. (must, rain)
d  There are three fire engines!
   (must, fire somewhere)
e  I don't know where Hannah is.
   (could, her bedroom)
f  My aunt isn't in the kitchen.
   (can't, cook dinner)
g  Whose coat is this? (might, John's)
h  We've won the lottery! (must, joke!)

**T.61**  Listen and check your answers.
Practise the stress and intonation in pairs.

## 3 What are they talking about?

Work in small groups.

1  **T.62**  Listen to five short conversations and guess the answer to the questions.

Example
A  It's Father's Day next Sunday.
B  I know. Shall we buy Dad a present or just send him a card?

Who do you think they are?
*They **must be** related. They **can't be** just friends. They **could be** husband and wife but they're **probably** brother and sister.*

a  Where do you think the people are? At home? In a restaurant? In a pub? In a hotel?
b  What do you think his job is? A sales manager? A bus driver? An actor? A taxi driver?
c  What do you think she's talking about? Visiting her parents? A first day in a new job? Meeting her boyfriend's parents? Her wedding day?
d  Who or what do you think they are talking about? A dog? The au pair? A horse? A baby?
e  What do you think they are doing? Swimming? Fishing? Rowing? Water-skiing?

2  Look at the photos. They are all of Verity and her family. Which is Verity? Who do you think the others are? Your teacher will tell you which group is closest.

## PRESENTATION (2)

## Modal verbs of probability in the past

1  **T.63a**  Poor Carl has had an accident. He is speaking to his friend, Andy, on the phone. In pairs, read and listen to Andy's side of the conversation. What do you think they are talking about? Use a dictionary to check any new words.

- Hi! Carl? It's Andy. Yeah. How are you? Feeling better?

- Really? Still using a crutch, eh? So you're not back at work yet?

- Two more weeks! That's when the plaster comes off, is it?

- No, I'm fine. The suntan's fading, though. Josie's is, too. She sends love, by the way.

- Yes, yes, I have. I got them back today. They're good. I didn't realize we'd taken so many.

- Yes, the sunset. It's a good one. All of us together on Bob and Marcia's balcony, with the mountains and the snow in the background. It's beautiful. Brings back memories, doesn't it?

- Yes, I know. I'm sorry. At least it was towards the end; it could have been the first day. You only came home two days early.

- Yes, we have. Yesterday, in fact. Bob wrote it and we all signed it. I don't know if it'll do any good, but it's worth a try.

- Yeah. They found it. It arrived on the next flight. Marcia was delighted.

- Sure. Some ups and downs, but generally I think we all got on well and had a great time. Shall we go again next year?

- Good! Great! It's a date. Next time look out for the trees! I'll ring again soon, Carl. Take care!

2 Tick (✓) the two sentences which you think are possible. Cross (✗) the one you think is not possible.

Example
What is the relationship between Andy and Carl?
- They must be friends. ✓
- They could be father and son. ✗
- They can't be business colleagues. ✓

a Where have they been?
- They must have been on holiday. ☐
- They can't have been somewhere sunny. ☐
- They might have been to Switzerland. ☐

b What happened to Carl?
- He must have broken his leg. ☐
- He could have broken his arm. ☐
- He must have come home early. ☐

c How many people went on holiday?
- There must have been at least five. ☐
- There might have been more than five. ☐
- There must have been three. ☐

d Where did they stay?
- They could have stayed on a campsite. ☐
- They must have stayed in a hotel. ☐
- They might have stayed with friends. ☐

e What did they do on holiday?
- They must have taken a lot of photos. ☐
- They could have been sunbathing. ☐
- They can't have been skiing. ☐

f What did Bob write?
- He might have written a letter to his wife. ☐
- He could have written a letter of complaint to the hotel. ☐
- He could have written a letter to the tour operator. ☐

g How did they travel?
- They must have flown. ☐
- They must have gone by train. ☐
- They might have hired a car. ☐

h What arrived on the next flight?
- It could have been Marcia's skis. ☐
- It must have been Marcia's suitcase. ☐
- It might have been Marcia's coat. ☐

3 Use some of the ideas in sentences a–h to say what you think happened to Andy and Carl.

Example
*Andy and Carl must be friends and they must have been on holiday together. They might…*

4 T.63b Listen to the full conversation between Andy and Carl. Which of your ideas were correct?

## ● Grammar questions

– What is the past of the following sentences?

| He | must<br>can't<br>could<br>might | be on holiday. |
| --- | --- | --- |

– What is the past of these sentences?
*I **must** buy some sunglasses.*
*I **have to** go home early.*
*I **can** see the sea from my room.*

# PRACTICE

## 1 Pronunciation and speaking

1 Work in pairs. Respond to the following situations using the word or words in brackets and the perfect infinitive (*have* + past participle). Take it in turns to read aloud and respond.

Example
**Student A**   I can't find my ticket. (must, drop)
**Student B**   *You must have dropped it.*

a John didn't come to school yesterday. (must, ill)
b Look at my new gold watch! (can't, buy yourself)
c Why is Isabel late for class? (might, oversleep)
d I can't find my homework. (must, forget)
e The teacher's checking Maria's work. (can't, finish already)
f Did you know that Charles got top marks in the exam? (must, cheat)
g Where's my umbrella? (could, leave it on the train)

2 **T.64**   Listen and check your answers. Do the exercise again paying particular attention to stress and intonation.

## 2 Discussing grammar

1 Fill in the gap in the second sentence with the modal verb in the past. Discuss your answers with a partner. (This exercise includes modal verbs of obligation and ability.)

a The pond is frozen. It *must* be very cold outside. (present probability)
You _____ very cold when you were out skiing. (past probability)

b You *must* do your homework tonight. (present obligation)
When I was at school we _____ homework every night. (past obligation)

c He *can't* be a member of the football team. He's hopeless at all sports! (present probability)
He _____ a member of his school football team. He was hopeless at all sports. (past probability)

d Jane *can* swim really well. (present ability)
She _____ really well when she was just eighteen months old. (past ability)

2 Work in pairs. Look at the list of modal auxiliary verbs. How many can you fit *naturally* into each gap? Discuss with your partner the differences in meaning.

| can | can't | could | must | might | shall | should |
|-----|-------|-------|------|-------|-------|--------|

a He _____ have been born during World War II.
b _____ you help me with the washing up, please?
c You _____ see the doctor immediately.
d It _____ be raining.
e _____ we go out for a meal tonight?
f I _____ stop smoking.
g It _____ have been Bill that you met at the party.
h I _____ learn to speak English.

# LANGUAGE REVIEW

## *must, could, might, can't*

1 *Must, could, might,* and *can't* are used to express degrees of probability about the present.

| | |
|---|---|
| *He **must be** in love.*<br>= very probable that he is in love | 95% sure |
| *He **could be** in love.*<br>*He **might be** in love.*<br>= possible, but less probable | 45% sure |
| *He **can't be** in love.*<br>= very probable that he is *not* in love | 95% sure |

2 They are used to express degrees of probability about the past (using the perfect infinitive).

*He **must have been** in love.*
= very probable that he was in love

*He **could have been** in love.*
*He **might have been** in love.*
= possible, but less probable

*He **can't have been** in love.*
= very possible that he was *not* in love

3 They can also be used with the continuous infinitive.

*You must **be joking**!*
*She could **be having** a shower.*
*It may/might **have been raining**.*

4 *May* can be used instead of *might* and *could*.

📖 **Grammar Reference: page 138.**

## VOCABULARY AND SPEAKING

Character adjectives

# What sort of person *are* you?

1. Are you usually smiling and happy? ❑
2. Do you enjoy the company of other people? ❑
3. Do you find it difficult to meet new people? ❑
4. Is it important to you to succeed in your career? ❑
5. Does your mood change often and suddenly for no reason? ❑
6. Do you notice other people's feelings? ❑
7. Do you think the future will be good? ❑
8. Can your friends depend on you? ❑
9. Is your room often in a mess? ❑
10. Do you get annoyed if you have to wait for anyone or anything? ❑
11. Do you put off until tomorrow what you could do today? ❑
12. Do you work hard? ❑
13. Do you keep your feelings and ideas to yourself? ❑
14. Do you often give presents? ❑
15. Do you talk a lot? ❑
16. Are you usually calm and not worried by things? ❑

Work in pairs.

1. Do the personality quiz above to discover what type of person you are. Use a dictionary to check any new words. Write **Y** for Yes, **N** for No, and **S** for Sometimes.

2. Ask your partner to do the quiz about you.
   Look at your ideas and your partner's ideas about you. Are they the same?

3. Match these adjectives with the questions in the quiz.

   | | | | |
   |---|---|---|---|
   | a | untidy    9 | i | lazy |
   | b | optimistic | j | generous |
   | c | sociable | k | moody |
   | d | talkative | l | hard-working |
   | e | reserved | m | easy-going |
   | f | shy | n | reliable |
   | g | impatient | o | cheerful |
   | h | ambitious | p | sensitive |

   Which are *positive* qualities and which are *negative*? Which could be both?

4. What is the opposite of each of the sixteen adjectives in Exercise 3?
   Remember that the prefixes *in-* and *un-* can sometimes be used to make negatives. Which of the adjectives above can use these?

5. Describe someone in the class to your partner but don't say who it is. Can your partner guess who it is?

## LISTENING AND SPEAKING

### *Brothers and sisters*

#### Pre-listening task

Do a class survey.

Find out who has any brothers and/or sisters. How many? Who has the most? Do they like having lots of brothers and sisters? Does anyone have a twin?
How many only children are there in the class? Do they like being an only child?

#### Listening and note-taking

T.65    Listen to two people talking about their families. First listen to Jillie, and answer the questions.

– How many brothers and sisters does she have?
– Was she happy as a child? Why? Why not?
– Is she happy now? Why? Why not?
– How has the family changed over the years?
– What do you learn about other members of her family and friends?

Now listen to Philippa and answer the same questions.

#### Discussion

– How many children do you have/would you like to have?
– What size is the perfect family?
– Would you like to have twins?

## READING AND SPEAKING

### Pre-reading task

Read the following quotation.

*'Only when the last tree has died and the last river has been poisoned and the last fish has been caught will we realize that we can't eat money.'*

Work in small groups. Who do you think said it?

a  A political leader.
b  A member of *Greenpeace*.
c  An American Indian.
d  An African fisherman.
e  A Greek philosopher.
f  A French farmer.

When do you think it was said?

a  In the 5th century BC.
b  In the 19th century.
c  In the 20th century.

Your teacher will give you the correct answer.

### Reading

You are going to read some extracts from a story by the French writer, Jean Giono (1895–1971), called *The Man Who Planted Trees*. In it Giono describes the world of a solitary shepherd who plants trees, while in the background there are two world wars.

**T.66a**  Read and listen to the extracts and answer the questions after each one.

## THE MAN WHO PLANTED TREES

### Extract 1

About forty years ago, I was taking a long trip on foot over mountain heights quite unknown to tourists. All around was barren and colourless land. Nothing grew there but wild lavender.

5   After five hours' walking I had still not found water. All about me was the same dryness, the same coarse grasses. I thought I saw in the distance a small black silhouette. It was a shepherd. Thirty sheep were lying about him on the baking earth. He gave me a
10  drink and took me to his cottage on the plain.

I felt peace in the presence of this man. I asked if I might rest here for a day. He found it quite natural—or, to be more exact, he gave me the impression that nothing could surprise him. I didn't
15  actually need to rest, but I was interested and wished to know more about him.

1  Giono wrote the story in 1953. In which year does the actual story begin?
2  The story takes place in France. Which part of France do you think it is? Why? What is the countryside like?
3  Why do you think the writer is interested in the shepherd? What do you think he likes about his lifestyle?

*The shepherd puts a large sack of acorns onto the table. He inspects each acorn and carefully chooses one hundred perfect ones before going to bed. The writer is curious. The next day when he goes out with the shepherd into the hills, he discovers what the acorns are for.*

**T.66b  Extract 2**

I noticed that he carried for a stick an iron rod as thick as my thumb and about a metre and a half long. He began thrusting his iron rod into the earth, making a hole in which he planted an acorn; then he refilled the hole. He was planting oak trees.  5

After the midday meal he resumed his planting. I suppose I must have been fairly insistent in my questioning, for he answered me. For three years he had been planting trees in this wilderness. He had planted one hundred thousand. Of the  10 hundred thousand, twenty thousand had sprouted. Of the twenty thousand he still expected to lose half. There remained ten thousand oak trees to grow where nothing had grown before.  15

That was when I began to wonder about the age of this man. He was obviously over fifty. Fifty-five he told me. His name was Elzéard Bouffier. I told him that in thirty  20 years his ten thousand oaks would be magnificent. He answered that if God granted him life, in another thirty years he would have planted so many more that these ten  25 thousand would be like a drop of water in the ocean.

The next day we parted.

4  How old do you think the writer was at the time of the story? A boy in his teens? In his twenties? Middle-aged? Older? Why?
5  How old will Elzéard be in thirty years time? What year will it be?
6  What do you think Elzéard's ambition is? What is his vision of the future?

*For the next five years the writer is a soldier and fights in World War I. The war ends in 1918 and his thoughts turn again to the tree-planter in the mountains. He returns to look for him.*

## T.66c  Extract 3

I had seen too many men die during those five years not to imagine easily that Elzéard Bouffier was dead, especially since, at twenty, one regards men of fifty as old men with nothing left to do but die. He
5 was not dead. As a matter of fact, he was extremely well. He had changed jobs. He had got rid of the sheep because they threatened his young trees. For, he told me, the war had disturbed him not at all. He had imperturbably continued to plant.

10    The oaks were then ten years old and taller than both of us. It was an impressive spectacle. I was literally speechless and, as he did not talk, we spent the whole day walking in silence through his forest. It measured eleven kilometres in length and
15 three kilometres at its greatest width. When you remembered that all this had come from the hands and the soul of this one man, you understood that men could be as effective as God in ways other than destruction.

7  Why did the writer think that Elzéard might have died?
8  How had the war affected Elzéard?
9  Why is the writer speechless?
10  What thoughts about human behaviour does he have in the last sentence?

*The writer returns for a final visit in 1945 after World War II. Elzéard is still alive. The writer is amazed at what he sees. Not only is there the forest, but many villages have been rebuilt, and by 1953 more than ten thousand people in the area owe their happiness to Elzéard Bouffier.*

## T.66d  Extract 4

The bus put me down in Vergons. In 1913 this village of ten or twelve houses had three inhabitants. All about them nettles were feeding upon the remains of abandoned houses. Now everything had changed.
5 Even the air. Instead of the harsh dry winds, a gentle breeze was blowing, laden with scents. A sound like water came from the mountains: it was the wind in the forest. Most amazing of all, I heard the actual sound of water falling into a pool. I saw a fountain
10 had been built. Ruins had been cleared away, and five houses restored. Now there were twenty-eight inhabitants, four of them young married couples. It was now a village where one would like to live.

When I think that one man was able to cause
15 this land of Canaan to grow from wasteland, I am convinced that in spite of everything, humanity is good.

Elzéard Bouffier died peacefully in his sleep in 1947.

11  What has happened in the writer's life that could have made him pessimistic?
   Is he in fact pessimistic about the world? Give a reason for your answer.
12  How is it that so many people owe their happiness to one man? What are the results of his tree-planting?
13  How old is Elzéard when he dies? Why is it so important that he had a long life?

## What do you think?

Work in groups.

1 Do you think the story about Elzéard is true?
Do you think Elzéard was ever married?

Give reasons for your opinions. Your teacher will tell you if you are correct.

2 How would you describe the personality of Elzéard Bouffier? Do you know any people like him in your life?

3 In the context of the twentieth century and its two world wars, what message is Giono trying to make about nature and the importance of individual human beings?

(This little book has been translated into over a dozen languages. Perhaps you could read the whole book in your own language, or better still, read it in English.)

## ● WRITING

### Sentence combination

1 Read the sentences about Elzéard Bouffier and then compare them with the paragraph below. Note the ways in which the sentences are combined.

Elzéard Bouffier was a shepherd.
He was poor.
He was solitary.
He lived in the mountains.
The mountains were barren.
They were in southern France.
Elzéard had a love of nature.
He had an incredible idea.
During his life he planted thousands of acorns.
The acorns grew into a forest of oak trees.
The forest made the countryside rich and fertile again.
He died when he was 89.

*Elzéard Bouffier was a poor, solitary shepherd, who lived in the barren mountains of southern France. His love of nature gave him an incredible idea. During his life he planted thousands of acorns. These grew into a forest of oak trees, which made the countryside rich and fertile again. Elzéard died when he was 89.*

2 Rewrite each group of sentences to form a more natural sounding paragraph.

a **A person**

Alan Higgins is a writer.
He is famous.
He is a millionaire.
He comes from the north of England.
He has gone to live in the USA.
He has written twenty-five novels.
His novels have been translated into five languages.
Hollywood is going to make a film of his latest novel.
The film will star Sunny Shaw.
Sunny Shaw's last film was a big box office hit. The film was called *Hot Night in the Snow*.

b **A place**

Oxford is a city.
It is a city in the south of England.
It is on the River Thames.
It has a population of about 100,000.
The city is famous.
It has one of the oldest universities in the world.
It has lots of other old buildings.
It has the Bodleian Library.
It has the Ashmolean Museum.
The Ashmolean was built in 1683.
Oxford was once the capital of England.
Not many people know this about Oxford.
Charles I made it the capital.
It was the capital from 1642–1645.

3 Write a short profile of a person (it could be you) and a place that are important to you.

## So do I! Neither do I!

1 Read the statements in the chart below. Complete the **You** column by putting (✓) if it is the same for you and (✗) if it isn't.

| | You | Polly | Polly's words |
|---|---|---|---|
| I want to travel the world. | | | |
| I don't want to have lots of children. | | | |
| I can speak four languages. | | | |
| I can't drive. | | | |
| I'm not going to marry until I'm 35. | | | |
| I went to America last year. | | | |
| I have never been to Australia. | | | |
| I don't like politicians. | | | |
| I am bored with the British Royal Family. | | | |
| I love going to parties. | | | |

2 **T.67** Listen to Polly. She is at a party and lots of friends are talking to her about themselves. Complete the **Polly** column by putting (✓) for what is the same and (✗) for what is not the same for Polly.

3 Listen again and write on the chart the *exact* words that Polly uses. Choose from the lists below.

| | | | | |
|---|---|---|---|---|
| So am I. | So do I. | So can I. | So did I. | So have I. |
| Neither am I. | Neither do I. | Neither can I. | Neither did I. | Neither have I. |
| I am. | I do. | I can. | I did. | I have. |
| I'm not. | I don't. | I can't. | I didn't. | I haven't. |

What does she say when it is the same for her?
What does she say when it is different?

📖 **Grammar Reference: page 138.**

4 Work in pairs.
Read out the statements in Exercise 1 to each other and give the correct response for you.

5 Go round the class.
Everyone must make a statement about themselves or give an opinion about something. The others in the class must respond.

Examples
**Student 1**    *I love chocolate ice cream!*
**Other students**    *So do I./Me too.*
    *I don't!*
**Student 2**    *I didn't do my homework.*
**Other students**    *Neither did I./Me neither.*
    *I did!*

# 10 Obsessions

Present Perfect Continuous
Time expressions
Complaining

## Test your grammar

1  For each pair, match a line in **A** with a line or picture in **B**.

| A | B |
|---|---|
| a What do you do<br>What are you doing | on your hands and knees?<br>for a living? |
| b She smokes<br>She's smoking | twenty cigarettes a day.<br>a Russian cigarette. |
| c He has<br><br>He's having | a bath. He can't come to the phone.<br>a lot of money. |
| d You're stupid.<br>You're being stupid. | You always are.<br>You aren't usually. |
| e Someone fired a gun.<br><br>Someone was firing a gun. |  |
| f The cat drowned.<br><br>The cat was drowning | so I jumped into the water and saved it.<br>It was terribly sad. |
| g What have you done with my headphones?<br>What have you been doing | I can't find them.<br>since I last saw you? |
| h Who has drunk my beer?<br><br>Who has been drinking my beer? |  |

2  Look at the second sentence of each pair. What do the verbs have in common?

## PRESENTATION (1)

### Present Perfect Continuous

1  Look at the newspaper headline and the picture of Peter.
–  What's Peter's job?
–  What has he passed?
–  'L' stands for *Learner*. What are L-plates on a car for?
–  What is he tearing up? Why?
–  Can you explain the play on words in the headline?

# Here endeth

## Young vicar passes driving test after 632 lessons over 17 years

VICAR Peter Newman is celebrating success — he has finally passed his driving test. He has been learning to drive for the past 17 years, and he
5 has had a total of 632 lessons.

Peter, 34, has spent over £9,000 on tuition, he has had eight different instructors, and he has crashed his car five times. Then, one week ago
10 he changed to an automatic car — and he passed his test immediately. He said last night, 'I've been praying for a driving-licence for over half my life, and at last my prayers have
15 been answered.'

2   **T.68**   Read and listen to the article. Then answer the questions.

– Why is Peter celebrating?
– Was it easy?
– What helped him to pass his test?
– What was his first accident?
– What was his big problem with driving?
– What has happened to his instructors? Why?
– Why hasn't he seen some of his relatives for so long?

3   Here are the answers to some questions. Write the questions using *he*. They all contain either the Present Perfect Simple or Continuous.

a   Seventeen years. (How long has he …?)
b   632. (How many …?)
c   Over £9,000. (How much …?)
d   Eight. (How many …?)
e   Five times. (How many times …?)
f   For over half his life. (How long …?)
g   That he would never pass. (What …?)
h   Fifty-six times. (How many …?)
i   By visiting relatives and people in the remote villages. (How …?)

**T.69**   Listen and check your answers.

# the Lessons

Peter, of St Andrew's Church, Repton in Nottinghamshire, began driving at the age of 17.

'It was in the country,' he said, 'and I was doing quite well until one morning, in a narrow lane, I saw a tractor coming towards me. I panicked and drove into a ten-foot hedge.'

Peter said, 'My big problem was confusing the clutch and the brake. I was absolutely hopeless. My instructors have been telling me for years that I would never pass, but I was determined to prove them wrong. Many of them have turned grey because of me!'

The turning-point came when Peter tried an automatic, and took his test again — for the fifty-sixth time.

He said, 'When I was told I'd passed, I went down on my knees and thanked God.'

So how has he been celebrating? 'I've been visiting all my relatives and people who live in the remote villages around here. I haven't seen some of them for years because I haven't been able to get to them. Now I can go anywhere!'

● **Grammar questions**

– Find the examples of the Present Perfect Simple and Continuous in the text.

– What is the difference between the Present Perfect Simple and Continuous?

*He **has been learning** to drive for 17 years.*
*He **has had** 632 lessons.*

– Which describes a *completed action*?

– Which describes an *activity over a period of time*?

## PRACTICE

### 1 Questions and answers

1   **T.70**   Listen to two people talking about driving and cars. Complete the questions.

a   _____ drive?
b   How long _____ ?
c   _____ a car?
d   How long _____ ?
e   How much _____ pay _____ ?
f   How many kilometres _____ ?
g   _____ ever _____ ?
h   Whose fault _____ ?

Ask and answer the same questions across the class.

2   Write a question with *How long …?* Use either the Present Perfect Simple or Continuous. If both are possible, use the Continuous.

a   I live in the country.       How long _____ ?
b   I play a lot of tennis.      How long _____ ?
c   I know Jack well.            How long _____ ?
d   I work in Prague.            How long _____ ?
e   I have an American car.      How long _____ ?

3   Make statements about yourself using the same verbs. In pairs, ask and answer questions with *How long …?*

4   For each of the sentences in Exercise 2, write another question in the Past Simple.

a   When _____ move there?
b   How old _____ when _____ started _____ ?
c   Where _____ meet _____ ?
d   Why _____ decide _____ ?
e   How much _____ pay _____ ?

## 2 Dialogues

T.71   Work in pairs and make dialogues. Listen to the example.

**Example**
A   tired – what ... doing?
B   exhausted – getting ready to go on holiday
A   done everything?
B   packed cases ... been to the bank ... haven't booked the taxi yet

A   *You look tired. What have you been doing?*
B   *I'm exhausted! I've been getting ready to go on holiday.*
A   *Have you done everything?*
B   *Well, I've packed the cases and I've been to the bank, but I haven't booked the taxi yet.*

a   A   covered in paint – what ... doing?
     B   decorating the bathroom
     A   finished yet?
     B   painted the door ... haven't put the wallpaper up yet

b   A   oil on your face – what ... doing?
     B   servicing the car
     A   done it yet?
     B   mended the lights ... haven't changed the oil yet

c   A   dirty hands – what ... doing?
     B   filthy – working in the garden
     A   finished now?
     B   cut the grass ... haven't watered the flowers yet

d   A   your eyes are red – what ... doing?
     B   exhausted – revising for my exams
     A   finished yet?
     B   done my chemistry and history ... haven't done any English yet

## 3 Discussing grammar

There is something wrong with the following sentences! Talk to a partner. Why are they strange? What would be better?

a   Ouch! I've been cutting my finger.
b   I've read Tolstoy's *War and Peace* this afternoon. It was a nice little read.
c   'Why is your hair wet?' 'I've swum.'
d   I'm terribly sorry, but I've been crashing into the back of your car.
e   You've got tears in your eyes. Why have you cried?

## PRESENTATION (2)

### Time expressions

1   Joanna Hardy is a writer. Look at the chart of events in her life. Answer the questions.

| Age | Events |
|-----|--------|
| 0 | Born 1950 |
| 5 | Started school |
| 6 | Wrote short stories about animals |
| 8 | Collection of poems published April 1958; visit to France and Germany |
| 11 | 16 Sept. 1961 mother died; visit to Italy |
| 15 | Wrote a novel (unpublished) |
| 18 | Went to Cambridge University for three years to read English literature |
| 19 | Met her first husband |
| 20 | Got married spring 1970 |
| 21 | Graduated 20 June 1971 First novel, *Chains*, published autumn 1971 |
| 22 | Daughter born 14 June 1972 |
| 25 | Novel *Strangers in the Night* published; won *The Times Literary Award* for best fiction |
| 29 | Divorce; visit to India and the Far East |
| 31 | Bought a house in north London |
| 33 | Novel *The Cry at Dawn* published |
| 35–37 | Made a series of TV programmes over a two-year period; met Jack, a BBC producer |
| 38 | Got married 10.30, 3 August 1988 to Jack; moved to her present address in Paris |
| 40 | Won *The Whitbread Trophy* for literary merit |
| 46 | Began her autobiography 1996 |
| Now | Still writing her autobiography |

a   Joanna has had an interesting life. What are some of the things she has done?
b   How long has she been writing?
c   What sort of things has she written?
d   How many novels has she written?
e   Has she won any prizes for her writing?
f   How long has she been married to Jack?
g   How many times has she been married?
h   How long has she been writing her autobiography?

2 Complete the sentences with words from the box.

> while she was at university    at the age of six
> since she married Jack         until she married Jack
> After the publication          between 1968 and 1971
> two years after she            while she was making
>   got married

a  She wrote her first stories _____ .
b  _____ of a collection of poems in 1958, she went to France and Germany.
c  She was at Cambridge University _____ .
d  She met her first husband _____ .
e  Her daughter was born _____ .
f  She met Jack _____ a series of TV programmes.
g  She lived in north London _____ .
h  She has been living in Paris _____ .

# PRACTICE

## 1 Questions and answers

Ask and answer the questions about Joanna Hardy.

a  When ... born?
b  When ... collection of poems published?
c  When ... mother die?
d  When ... get married for the first time?
e  When ... graduate?
f  When ... daughter born?
g  When ... India and the Far East?
h  When ... for the second time?
i  How long ... first marriage last?
j  How long ... in Paris?

T.72   Listen and check your answers.

## 2 *How long are you here for?*

1  Joanna is on a two-week tour of the United States. Look at her itinerary.

|       | Week 1    | Week 2      |
|-------|-----------|-------------|
| Sun   | New York  | Kansas City |
| Mon   | New York  | Kansas City |
| Tues  | Boston    | Dallas      |
| Wed   | Boston    | Denver      |
| Thurs | Cleveland | Los Angeles |
| Fri   | Chicago   | Los Angeles |
| Sat   | Chicago   | Fly home    |

2  It is Monday of the second week, and she is at a press conference. How does she answer these questions?

> How long are you in the States for?

> How long have you been in the States?

> When do you go back to England?

> Where were you the day before yesterday?

> Where were you this time last week?

> Where will you be the day after tomorrow?

T.73   Listen and check your answers.

3  Imagine you are on tour for two weeks. Write your itinerary. Decide what day it is and where you are. In pairs, ask and answer the same questions.

## 3 Discussing grammar

Work in pairs.

1  Correct the mistakes in the questions.

a  What time did you go to bed at last night?
b  What did you do the last weekend?
c  What are you doing this night?
d  When this lesson begin?
e  When ends this lesson?
f  Are you going to study English the next month?
g  When you born?
h  What's today date?

2  Ask and answer the questions above.

## LANGUAGE REVIEW

### Present Perfect Continuous

The Present Perfect Continuous relates past activities to the present. It has two main uses.

1  To express unfinished past.
   *I've been working here for fifteen years.*
   *How long have you been learning English?*

   Remember the verbs that rarely take the continuous.
   *I've known Jack for years and years.*
   *How long have you had your car?*

2  To express the present result of past activities.
   *You look tired. What have you been doing?*
   *I've been doing my homework.*

### Time expressions

See the Grammar Reference section, page 139.

📖  **Grammar Reference: page 138.**

## ● READING

### Pre-reading task

1 Work in pairs. Which of the following do you think is the riskiest?

> playing Russian roulette     hang-gliding
> taking cocaine               smoking tobacco
> riding a motorbike at 200 kph
> crossing the road with your eyes closed

2 Read the quotations about smoking. What view of smoking does each quotation express?

a 'Out of a thousand smokers of 20 cigarettes a day, one will be murdered, six will be killed on the roads, and about three hundred and thirty will die prematurely because of their smoking.'

b 'If you decide to give up smoking and drinking, you don't actually live longer; it just seems longer.'

c 'Teenagers begin to smoke because they think it's cool and because they think they look grown-up. The cigarette is a symbol of defiance and an attack on authority.'

d 'I have every sympathy with the American who was so horrified by what he had read about the effects of smoking that he gave up reading.'

e 'The world spends $150 billion a year on smoking-related illnesses.'

3 Have attitudes to smoking changed in your country over the past few years? How? Do as many people smoke?

4 You are going to read an interview with a man called B J Cunningham. Look at the pictures and read these facts about him.

> He's a chain smoker.
> He wears black leather cowboy clothes.
> He rides a Harley-Davidson motorbike.
> He has a weak chest.
> He returned to his true love after six months.
> He has started his own tobacco company.
> His company is not very successful.
> He smoked fifteen cigarettes during the interview.

- How old do you think he is?
- What do you know about his way of life?
- What kind of a man do you think he is?
- What nationality do you think he is?
- Would you like to meet him?

## Reading

Read the text.
Were your ideas about B J Cunningham correct?
Did you learn anything about him that surprised you?

# 'Here! Have one of mine!'
## 'Death cigarettes? You must be joking!'

**David Andrews meets B J Cunningham, a dedicated smoker who loyally puffs his own cigarettes called *Death*.**

OK. So here are the facts. There's an Englishman called B J Cunningham who has been smoking since he was eleven. He's a chain smoker who's in love with smoking. He smokes between two and three packets a day, and already, at the age of 30, has a weak chest. He was in hospital for six days when his lungs collapsed. 'It was at that point that I did actually give up cigarettes for six months.' But then he returned to his true love. He wears black leather cowboy clothes and has a fondness for classic Harley-Davidson motorbikes, which he has been riding for the past fifteen years. 'I've had about ten of them,' he says coolly.

So far, not a very remarkable life. But then, B J Cunningham (no one actually knows what B J stands for) had an idea one night in a bar in LA. 'Let's market a cigarette called *Death*,' he said to a business partner. 'Why?' said the partner.

'It's obvious,' he explains to me. 'When you take a packet of cigarettes out of your top pocket and put it on the bar in front of you, you're making a statement about yourself, exactly as you do with the clothes you wear, the music you like, and the newspaper you read. You're saying, "These cigarettes are a part of me."'

'So, if you take out a packet of Benson and Hedges, you're saying, "I'm classy — gold packet — part of high society." If you take out a packet of Marlboro, you're saying, "I'm an outdoor type, I like wearing a cowboy hat and riding horses …"'

'Now, if you produce a packet of *Death* cigarettes,' he continues, producing a packet of *Death* cigarettes to illustrate his point, 'what you're saying is …'

He looks at me to make sure that I'm going to write down what you're saying about yourself if you smoke *Death* cigarettes. But do I need to? We all know what *Death* cigarettes are about. B J Cunningham has been telling us about them since he started his Enlightened Tobacco Company (ETC) in 1991.

Everyone has now got the joke, thank you very much. We've seen the black packets with their death's head on the front and the white packets which are called *Death Lights*; and we've heard about the coffin-shaped vending machines in pubs and clubs.

However, for anyone who has managed to avoid B J's publicity, here goes. *Death* cigarettes are for the smoker who wants to say, 'Yes, I'm killing myself, but at least I know it, and I smoke a brand which doesn't try to hide the fact.' '*Death* cigarettes,' concludes B J, 'say, "Don't you dare tell me to stop!"'

B J Cunningham, now on his ninth cigarette of the interview, says he wants to expose the hypocrisy behind the tobacco industry. Governments can't afford to ban smoking because they receive huge amounts of money in tax. Tobacco companies try to improve their image by sponsoring sports events such as motor racing, rugby, football, cricket, and tennis, at vast expense. 'What everybody wants to forget is that smoking kills. That's why I'm here, to remind people that smoking and death are linked.'

The ETC hoped to win a good share of the UK market. 'Cigarettes in Britain are a £12 billion industry in which four companies control 95% of the market. The question is: How do we get a share?' He knows the question but he can't afford the answer. The ETC can't afford to advertise like the big companies. It has been losing about £1 million a year.

Personally, I have a very different opinion as to why so few people choose to smoke a brand of cigarette called *Death*. B J Cunningham has misunderstood human psychology. Of course smokers *know* that their habit is probably going to kill them, but they prefer not to think about it. The only people who are going to smoke his cigarettes are people like himself. When I offered one to a friend recently, his reaction was, 'You must be joking.' And this is what *Death* cigarettes are all about. It's a joke that was funny, but isn't funny any more.

But B J is still obsessed by fags. 'Do you know the main reason I love my job?' he says. 'It's because it gives me a chance to attack the anti-smoking killjoys! Those puritans who try to control our lives. I've met many people who don't smoke, but who tell me that if smoking were made illegal, they would fight it. You just can't have laws which control every aspect of the way people live.'

I finally started to warm to this character B J Cunningham. It was the end of the interview, and the number of fag ends in the ashtray had increased to fifteen. Perhaps he had something important to say after all. Not just, 'Hey, everybody! Look at me! I'm weird, and I'm killing myself!'

## Comprehension check

Read the text more carefully. Complete the sentences with the best ending, a, b, or c.

1  B J Cunningham smokes two or three packets of cigarettes a day …
a  even though he has a weak chest.
b  because he has to for his job.
c  to prove that smoking is safe.

2  He wears cowboy clothes and rides a Harley-Davidson motorbike because …
a  he plays in a rock 'n' roll band.
b  he likes everything that comes from the States.
c  it is part of the image he wants to create for himself.

3  B J Cunningham says that smokers choose a certain brand of cigarettes …
a  because it shows the kind of person they are.
b  to go with the clothes they are wearing.
c  because they want to be sporty or part of high society.

4  We get the impression that the interviewer …
a  likes and admires B J Cunningham.
b  is bored and irritated by B J Cunningham.
c  is very angry with B J Cunningham.

5  B J Cunningham says *Death* cigarettes are for people …
a  who want to be honest and aggressive.
b  who want to prove that smoking cigarettes doesn't kill.
c  who want to expose the hypocrisy of governments and the tobacco industry.

6  B J Cunningham says that his job …
a  is to get sponsorship for sports events.
b  is to sell as many cigarettes as he can.
c  is to be honest about the dangers of smoking.

7  The interviewer thinks that the ETC hasn't been successful because …
a  the big tobacco companies spend £12 billion on advertising.
b  everybody thinks that *Death* cigarettes are just a joke.
c  smokers don't want to be reminded that smoking kills.

8  B J Cunningham …
a  wants to defend people's right to smoke.
b  wants to control the lives of smokers.
c  thinks that smoking will one day be made illegal.

9  The interviewer warms to B J Cunningham at the end of the interview …
a  when B J Cunningham gives his main reason for selling *Death* cigarettes.
b  because he realizes that he is just a weird eccentric.
c  when he finally puts out his last cigarette.

## Language work

Here are the answers to some questions. Write the questions.

1  _____ ?
Since he was eleven.

2  _____ ?
Between forty and sixty.

3  _____ ?
Yes, he has. He gave up for six months after his lungs collapsed.

4  _____ ?
For fifteen years.

5  _____ ?
About ten.

6  _____ ?
In 1991.

7  _____ ?
About £1 million a year.

8  _____ ?
Fifteen.

## Discussion

Discuss the following in small groups. Then report back to the whole class.

1  How much is a packet of cigarettes in your country? How much of that is tax?
What sort of health warnings are there?
Do tobacco companies sponsor any sports events?

2  Why is it that drugs such as nicotine and alcohol are legal in many countries, while other drugs are illegal?

3  Do you think smoking should be banned in all public places? Or, should smokers be allowed to smoke when and where they want?

# ● VOCABULARY AND PRONUNCIATION

## Compound nouns

1 The following are definitions of words from Unit 10. What are the words?

**Example**
What you wear if you want to listen to your Walkman.
*Headphones.*

a The piece of paper that means you can drive a car.
b What you have to pass to get the piece of paper!
c What you put on the walls of your house when you decorate a room.
d An interview given to a lot of journalists to make an announcement.
e Someone who smokes one cigarette after another.
f Someone that you run a business with.
g Where smokers put out their cigarettes.

What do you notice about these words?

2 Nouns can be combined to make a new word. These are called **compound nouns**. They are written in different ways.

| | |
|---|---|
| *postcard*<br>*postbox*<br>*postman*<br>*postcode* | One word. |

| | |
|---|---|
| *post office* | Two words. |

Occasionally the words are hyphenated (*window-shopping*). There are no rules, and English people themselves often have to go to a dictionary to check the spelling.

**T.74** Listen to the words. Where is the stress?

3 Put one word in each box to form three compound nouns. Look at the example. Check the spelling in a dictionary.

| a | *tooth* | ache<br>brush<br>paste | i | _____ | conditioning<br>mail<br>port |
|---|---|---|---|---|---|
| b | dining<br>living<br>changing | _____ | j | _____ | cup<br>spoon<br>pot |
| c | _____ | lights<br>warden<br>jam | k | _____ | glasses<br>bathing<br>set |
| d | _____ | way<br>racing<br>bike | l | news<br>travel<br>estate | _____ |
| e | cookery<br>telephone<br>note | _____ | m | wrapping<br>writing<br>toilet | _____ |
| f | _____ | engine<br>place<br>works | n | chair<br>fire<br>dust | _____ |
| g | birthday<br>credit<br>get-well | _____ | o | _____ | centre<br>basket<br>spree |
| h | _____ | dresser<br>brush<br>cut | p | _____ | case<br>shop<br>worm |

4 Work in pairs.
Look up the words below in your dictionary and find more compound nouns. Write some sentences like those in Exercise 1 to test the other students in the class. Look up these words.

hand     head     night     snow     eye     back     land

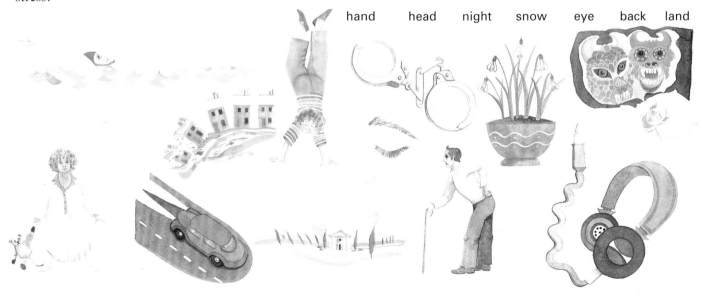

● LISTENING AND SPEAKING

# Collectors

## Pre-listening task

1 What kinds of things do people often collect?

2 Do you collect anything? Did you use to when you were younger?

## Listening

You are going to listen to two people who are both keen collectors. Divide into two groups.

Look at the picture about your person. What can you see? What does she/he collect? What questions would you like to ask her/him? Listen and answer the questions.

### Group A

T.75a    Listen to Margaret Tyler. She lives in Wembley, north London. Her children have now grown up and left home, and so she lives alone with her incredible collection.

### Group B

T.75b    Listen to Ted Hewitt. He lives with his wife and three small children in Chorleywood, a village between London and Oxford. He owns a coach business.

## Comprehension check

1 Where does she/he live? Who with?
2 What does she/he do for a living?
3 How big is her/his collection?
4 How long has she/he been collecting?
5 How many rooms of the house are taken up with the collection?
6 What's her/his favourite piece?
7 How much has the collection cost?
8 Where do the pieces come from?
9 Is she/he in touch with other people who share the same hobby?
10 What ambitions does she/he have?

When you have answered the questions, find a partner from the other group. Compare and swap information.

## Guessing game

Your teacher will tell one student what he or she collects. The others must ask questions to find out what it is.

How big are they?          Can you buy them?

When you've guessed what it is, ask some of the questions in the Comprehension check above.

How long have you been collecting?

## ● WRITING

### Beginning and ending letters

1 Match the correct beginning and ending for the five letters on the right. Which letter …

… asks for information? … accepts an invitation?
… invites? … gives news?
… says that money has been received?

2 Which of these sentences continues each letter?

a Could you please send me your brochure and a price list? I would be most grateful.
b I've changed my job a few times since I last spoke to you, and as you know, I've moved, too.
c Unfortunately this amount did not include packing and postage, which is £7.50.
d June and I are having a barbecue with all our friends, and we were wondering if you could come.
e We'd love to come. I haven't been to your part of the country for ages.

3 Note the following points about formal and informal letters.

- We can write contractions (*I've*, *we're*, *I'll*) in an informal letter, but not in a formal one.
- All letters begin with *Dear* …
- You can end an informal letter with *Best wishes* or *Love*.

Here are some useful phrases for informal letters:

**Beginning**
*It was lovely to hear from you. I was pleased to hear that …*
*Thank you for your letter. I was sorry to hear that …*
*I'm sorry I haven't written before, but …*
*This is just a note to say …*

**Giving news**
*We're having a lovely time in …*
*I've been very busy recently. Last week I … and next week I'm going to …*

**Ending**
*I'm looking forward to seeing you …/to hearing from you soon.*
*Give my regards to Robert …*
*Write to me soon …*
*I hope to hear from you soon …*
*Write and tell me when …*

4 Write a letter to a friend who you haven't been in touch with for a long time. Give your news, describe some things that you have done recently, and say what your future plans are. Ask about his/her news and family. Try to arrange to meet somewhere. Remember to put your address and the date in the top right-hand corner of your letter.

### Beginnings

a Dear Mary

This is just a note to ask if you and Dave are free on the evening of July 11.

b Dear Jane

Many thanks for your letter. It was lovely to hear from you after such a long time. You asked me what I've been doing. Well, …

c Dear Sir/Madam

I saw an advertisement in the Daily Telegraph for weekend breaks at your hotel.

d Dear Peter

Thank you so much for inviting Dave and me to your summer party.

e Dear Mr Smith

We received your order for the *World Encyclopaedia* on CD ROM, and your cheque for £75.

### Endings

1 Many thanks. I look forward to hearing from you in the near future.

Yours faithfully

James Fox

2 We will have pleasure in meeting your order as soon as we can.

Yours sincerely

Thames Valley Computer Software

3 It would be lovely to meet some time. Do you ever come to London? You must let me know.

Love

4 Do get in touch soon and tell me if you can make it.

Regards to you all.

Best wishes

5 We're really looking forward to seeing you again, and to meeting your friends.

Best wishes

*Mary*

## Complaining

1 Choose a word or words from the box to complete the sentences. Some are used more than once.

| | | | |
|---|---|---|---|
| too much | a few | any | How many |
| as much as | How much | some | too many |
| as many as | enough | a little | |

a '_____ cigarettes do you smoke a day?'
'Forty.'
'That's _____ . You shouldn't smoke _____ at all.'

b '_____ alcohol do you drink?'
'About a bottle of wine a day.'
'That's _____ . You shouldn't drink _____ that.'

c '_____ do you weigh?'
'Sixteen and a half stone.'
'That's _____ . You should try to lose _____ weight.'

d '_____ do you earn?'
'Not _____ money to pay all my bills!'

e '_____ people are there in your class?'
'Forty.'
'I think that's _____ .'

f '_____ aspirins do you take when you have a headache?'
'About ten or twelve.'
'That's _____ . You mustn't take _____ that!'

g 'How old are you?'
'Seventeen. I'm old _____ to get married, but I'm not old _____ to vote!'

h 'When did you last go to the cinema?'
'Quite recently. Just _____ days ago.'

i 'Do you take sugar in your coffee?'
'Just _____ .'

2 In pairs, ask and answer the same questions.

3 Write a dialogue of complaint, either in a restaurant, a hotel, or a clothes shop. Act it out to the rest of the class.

Example

| Waiter | Lady |
|---|---|
| *How was your meal, madam?* | *It was terrible. The soup was too salty, the steak wasn't cooked enough, and there weren't enough vegetables. The table was too noisy and the waiters were slow.* |
| *But apart from that?* | *It was fine, thanks.* |

# Tell me about it!

Indirect questions
Question tags
Informal language

---

**1** T.76 Look at the picture. Read and listen to the story.

**The Tramp**

A tramp was sleeping on a park bench late at night. A man and woman were walking past. One of them tapped him on the shoulder and asked, 'Excuse me! What's the time?' The tramp was very annoyed at being woken up. 'I don't know!' he said angrily. 'I haven't got a watch.' And he went back to sleep.

Some time later another man was passing. He woke the tramp up and said, 'I'm sorry to bother you, but I wonder if you could tell me what time it is.'

Again the tramp said that he didn't know. By now he was very fed up, so he got a pen and a piece of paper and wrote I DON'T KNOW WHAT THE TIME IS on it, and went back to sleep.

Half an hour later, a policeman was passing. He read the sign, woke the tramp up and said, 'It's 2.30, sir.'

**2** Correct these sentences.

\*I wonder if you could tell me ~~what time is it~~.
\*I don't know ~~what's the time~~.

## PRESENTATION (1)

### Indirect questions

1 T.77 Rosie has just arrived at the railway station of a strange town. She goes to the tourist office to get some information.

Look at the information she wants, then listen to the dialogue. Complete her sentences.

| **What Rosie wants to know** | **What Rosie says** |
|---|---|
| a Could you help me? | I wonder _____ |
| b What time do the banks close? | I don't know _____ |
| c How old is this town? | Have you any idea _____ ? |
| d Are we near the centre of town? | I'm not sure _____ |
| e Which hotel did you suggest? | I can't remember _____ |

### ● Grammar questions

– How does the word order change in indirect questions?
– What happens to *do/does/did* in indirect questions?
– What do we use if there is no question word (*where? how old? what time?*)?

2 In pairs, practise the conversation. How much can you remember?

3 Here is some more information that Rosie wants. Use the prompts to ask indirect questions.

a When was the town founded? (Could you tell me …?)

b What's the population of the town? (Do you know …?)

c Where can I change some money? (I'd like to know …)

d What's the exchange rate today? (Do you happen to know …?)

e Is there a dry cleaner's near here? (I wonder …)

f Where is there a cheap place to eat? (Have you any idea …?)

g How long does it take to get to the centre of town from here? (Can you tell me …?)

h Did it rain here yesterday? (Do you remember …?)

4 In pairs, ask and answer similar indirect questions about the town where you are now.

## PRACTICE

### 1 *We can't hear what she's saying!*

1 **T.78** Listen to the radio news. Unfortunately the reception is bad, and there are some things you can't hear. What don't you know?

Example
We don't know
We've no idea     | *what time the*
I couldn't hear   | *train crash*
I'm not sure      | *happened.*

2 Your teacher has the information. Ask the direct questions.

## 2 Speaking

1 *Madame Tussaud's Waxworks* is London's most popular tourist attraction. What do you know about it?

Make statements about *Madame Tussaud's* using the prompts.

I wonder …              I haven't a clue …
I'd love to know …      Does anybody know …

Example
*where … born*
*I wonder where she was born.*

a where Madame Tussaud … (come) from
b when … alive
c how … (learn) to make things in wax
d which countries … (live) in
e … married
f … children
g why … (go) to England
h when the Waxworks … (open) in London
i how many people a year … (visit) the Waxworks

2 Work in pairs. Your teacher will give you some information about Madame Tussaud, but you will not have the same information. Ask and answer questions to complete the information. Use both direct and indirect questions.

Example

**Student A**
Marie Tussaud was born in Strasbourg in 1761. Her father died … (*When?*), and her family moved to Switzerland.

**Student B**
Marie Tussaud was born in Strasbourg in 1761. Her father died two months before she was born, and her family moved to … (*Where?*)

> Do you know when her father died?

> He died two months before she was born.

> To Switzerland.

> Where did her family move to?

## 3 Asking polite questions

1 Match a word in **A** with a line in **B** and a line in **C**.

| A | B | C |
|---|---|---|
| What | football team | times have you been on a plane? |
| | newspaper | does it take you to get ready in the morning? |
| | colour | do you support? |
| | long | shoes do you take? |
| Which | size | of car have you got? |
| | flavour | do you read? |
| | far | ice-cream is your favourite? |
| How | sort | is it to the station from here? |
| | many | time do you spend watching TV? |
| | much | eyes have you got? |

2 Indirect questions can be more polite than direct questions. In pairs, ask and answer indirect questions using the ideas in Exercise 1.

Example

> Could you tell me which football team you support?

> Would you mind telling me what size shoes you take?

---

# PRESENTATION (2)

## Question tags

1 **T.79** Look at the picture and listen to Jessie (J), aged 3, talking to her mother, Sarah (S).

J Mummy?
S Yes, Jessie?
J I've got ten fingers, haven't I?
S Yes, that's right, my darling. Ten lovely little fingers.
J And my brother's called Joe, isn't he?
S Yes, he is. He's at school at the moment.
J And Daddy went to work this morning, didn't he?
S Yes, he went in his big blue car.
J And we don't like tigers, do we, Mummy?
S Well, they're beautiful, but they're dangerous, it's true.
J Can I have a biscuit now, Mummy?

● **Grammar questions**

– Jessie *knows* that she has ten fingers, and she *knows* that her brother's called Joe. So she's not really asking questions. What *is* she doing?

– How do we make question tags?

2 Look at the dialogue between Caroline Bailey (C) and her secretary, Norma (N). Fill each gap with the correct question tag. Choose from the box.

| didn't I? | aren't I? | isn't it? |
|---|---|---|
| am I? | haven't I? | does it? |

C Now, what's happening today? I've got a meeting this afternoon, _____ ?
N Yes, that's right. With Henry and Ted.
C And the meeting's here, _____ ?
N No, it isn't. It's in Ted's office, at 3.00.
C Oh! I'm not having lunch with anyone, _____ ?
N No, you're free all morning.
C Phew! I'll start on that report, then. Er ... I signed all my letters, _____ ?
N No, you didn't, actually. They're on your desk, waiting for you.
C Ah, right! And tomorrow I'm going to Scotland, _____ ?
N Yes. You're booked on the early morning shuttle.
C OK. It doesn't leave until 8.00, _____ ?
N 8.15, to be precise.
C Gosh, Norma! Where would I be without you?

**T.80** Listen and check your answers.

● **Grammar questions**

– Did the intonation of Jessie's question tags go up or down? What about Caroline's?

– Whose use of question tags means, 'I'm not sure so I'm checking'? Whose use of question tags means, 'Please talk to me'?

# PRACTICE

## 1 Grammar and intonation

1 Look at the sentences and complete the question tags.

| | |
|---|---|
| a It isn't very warm today, | *is it?* ▼ |
| b The weather forecast was wrong again, | |
| c You can cook, | |
| d You don't eat snails, | |
| e You've got a CD, | |
| f Sally's very clever, | |
| g There are a lot of people here, | |
| h The film wasn't very good, | |
| i I am a silly person, | |
| j You aren't going out dressed like that, | |

2 **T.81a** Listen and check your answers. Put ▼ if the tag falls and ▲ if it rises.

3 Match one of the following responses with a sentence in Exercise 1.

☐ Yes. She's as bright as a button.

☐ Believe it or not, I haven't. I've got a tape recorder, though.

☐ Why? What's wrong with it? I thought I looked really smart.

☐ Yuk! No, I don't! They're disgusting!

☐ No, it's freezing.

☐ No, you're not. Just because you made one mistake doesn't mean you're silly.

☐ Me? No! I can't even boil an egg.

☐ Yes! It always is, though, isn't it?

☐ I know! It's absolutely packed! I can't move!

☐ Terrible! The worst I've seen for ages.

**T.81b** Listen and check your answers. In pairs, practise the dialogues.

## 2 Conversations

Work in pairs.

1 Your teacher will give you a dialogue. Decide where you think question tags could go, what they are, and whether they fall or rise.

2 Learn the dialogue by heart. Act it out to the rest of the class.

3 **T.82** Listen and check your answers. Are your ideas the same?

# LANGUAGE REVIEW

## Indirect questions

1 Indirect questions are introduced with expressions such as the following.

*I don't know …*
*I wonder …*
*Could you tell me …?*
*I'm not sure …*

2 Indirect questions have the same word order as the positive, and there is no *do/does/did*.

*I don't know **where he went**.*
*I wonder **if she's arrived** yet.*
*Could you tell me **what the answer is**?*
*I'm not sure **how much it costs**.*

## Question tags

The meaning of a question tag depends on how you say it.

1 A question tag with a falling intonation isn't really a question at all. It is a way of making conversation by asking the listener to agree with the speaker.

*It's a lovely day, **isn't it**?*
*We didn't play very well today, **did we**?*

2 A question tag with a rising intonation is more like a real question. It means 'I think I'm right, but can you confirm it for me?'

*Our train leaves at 7.00, **doesn't it**?*
*You haven't lost the keys, **have you**?*

📖 **Grammar Reference: page 139.**

## ● VOCABULARY AND IDIOMS

## Do you know what your body can do?

Use your dictionary to check any new words.

1 As a class, brainstorm all the parts of the body that you know. Fill the board with all that you can think of.

2 Work in pairs and say which parts of the body you use to do the following things.

| | | | | | |
|---|---|---|---|---|---|
| kick | bite | hit | climb | chew | drop |
| hold | hug | kiss | lick | point | scratch |
| tie | kneel | think | pat | blow | clap |
| stare | whistle | | | | |

3 Which verbs go with which nouns and phrases?
Match a line in **A** with a line in **B**.

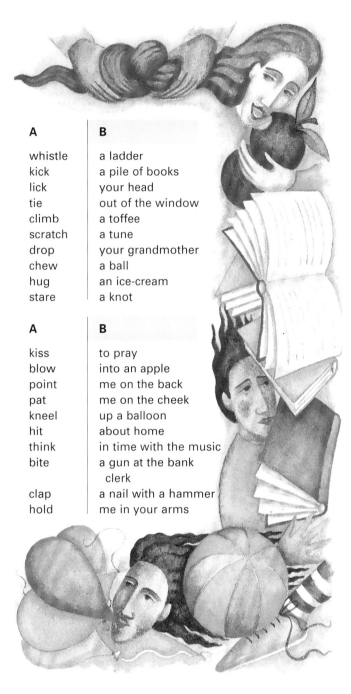

| A | B |
|---|---|
| whistle | a ladder |
| kick | a pile of books |
| lick | your head |
| tie | out of the window |
| climb | a toffee |
| scratch | a tune |
| drop | your grandmother |
| chew | a ball |
| hug | an ice-cream |
| stare | a knot |

| A | B |
|---|---|
| kiss | to pray |
| blow | into an apple |
| point | me on the back |
| pat | me on the cheek |
| kneel | up a balloon |
| hit | about home |
| think | in time with the music |
| bite | a gun at the bank clerk |
| clap | a nail with a hammer |
| hold | me in your arms |

4 Many of the verbs above form interesting idioms.
How many of the following do you know or can you
guess? Check the others in your dictionary.

to drop someone a line
to kick the habit
to think the world of someone
to kiss something goodbye
to blow your own trumpet
to hit the roof
to hold your breath

5 Complete the gaps with one of the idioms in Exercise
4. If necessary, change the form of the verb. The first
letter of each missing word is given.

a The best way to stop hiccups is to h _____ your
b _____ and count to ten.

b My parents h_____ the r_____ when I said I'd
been to an all-night party.

c I've tried so many times to stop biting my nails, but I
just can't k_____ the h_____ .

d I've never seen a couple so in love. They clearly
t_____ the w_____ of each other.

e When my teenage daughter learnt to drive, I had to
buy her a car or k_____ my own car g_____!

f Tell your brother to stop b_____ his own t_____ .
We don't want to hear how wonderful he thinks he is!

g D_____ me a l_____ when you know what time
you're coming, and I'll meet you at the station.

## ● READING AND SPEAKING

### How well do you know your world?

### Pre-reading task

1 Work in small groups.
How many of the following questions can you answer?

– Why do women live longer than men?
– What man-made things on Earth can be seen from
  space?
– How many new words enter the English language
  every year?
– Why is walking under ladders thought to be unlucky?
– Why are horseshoes believed to be lucky?
– Why is the expression 'Mayday' used as a distress call?
– Why do they drive on the left in Britain and on the
  right in other countries?
– What is the biggest office in the world?
– How clever are dolphins?

2 Preface each question above with one of the following
according to what is true for you. Remember the word
order for making indirect questions.

I think I know ...    I'm not sure ...    I don't know ...
I've no idea ...      I wonder ...

3 Discuss your answers as a class. Which of the
questions interest you most? Why?

## Reading

The questions in the Pre-reading task were all sent in to a science magazine. Read the answers to the questions. How much of the information did your class already know?

# You ask
# ... we answer!

**Q** ## Why do women live longer than men?

**A** Women generally live about six years longer than men. Evidence suggests that boys are the weaker sex at birth, which means that more die in infancy. Also women do not have as much heart disease as men. In terms of lifestyle, men smoke more than women and thus more die of smoking-related diseases. They drink more and are more aggressive in behaviour, particularly when driving cars, so they are more likely to die in accidents. Also, they generally have more dangerous occupations, such as building work.

Historically, women died in childbirth and men in wars. Hence nuns and philosophers often lived to great ages. Now, childbearing is less risky and there are fewer wars. The country with the highest life expectancy is Japan, where the average age for men is 76 and for women 82.

Morimoto, the oldest living man in the world (1877 – )

**Q** ## What man-made things on Earth can be seen from space?

**A** *'When men first flew in space, they were amazed to discover that the only man-made object visible from orbit was the Great Wall of China.'* This is a nice idea, but it's not true. The Great Wall is mostly grey stone in a grey landscape and, in fact, is very difficult to see even from an aeroplane flying at a mere 15 kilometres above. What can be seen when orbiting the earth (from about 200 kilometres up) are the fires of African desert people, and the lights of fishing boats off Japan; also, a very long wire fence in Western Australia which marks farmland on one side and desert on the other.

**Q** ## Why is walking under ladders believed to be unlucky?

**A** *There are a few explanations for this. The most common is that someone on the ladder might be holding a pot of paint or a bucket of water which could drop on you if you walked underneath. Another explanation relates to the Tyburn gallows at what is now Marble Arch in London. Until 1783 criminals climbed a ladder to the gallows with a rope round their neck and this was then kicked from under them. The belief grew that walking under a ladder invited death.*

**Q** ## Why is the expression 'Mayday' used as a distress call?

**A** The term 'Mayday' is the internationally recognized radio telephone signal of distress. It is only used when a ship is in great danger and needs help immediately. The signal is transmitted on a wavelength of 2,182 kHz, which is permanently monitored by rescue services on the shore. The use of the expression has a very straightforward explanation. It simply came from the French phrase 'm'aidez', which means 'help me'. It was officially adopted internationally in 1927.

**Q** ## How many new words enter the English language every year?

**A** Unfortunately no list is kept. In France there is the Académie Française which approves new words but in England there are only dictionaries. The most authoritative of these is the *Oxford English Dictionary* (OED) which has 20 volumes, but this does not make rules about the language. It simply records the development of English worldwide as best it can. It accepts about 4000 new words (or new meanings) every year. The OED has readers in all English-speaking parts of the world, who record repeated uses of new words, including numerous technical terms. Some words take a surprisingly long time to enter the OED. For example 'acid rain' was first used in 1859, but its usage was rare for over 100 years and it didn't appear in the dictionary until the 1980s.

**Q** ## What is the world's biggest office?

**A** The Pentagon is the largest office in the world. This famous five-sided building, which is the US Department of Defense, was built in just 16 months during World War II, in Arlington, Virginia. It is designed to hold up to 40,000 people. It has 28 kilometres of corridors, 7,754 windows, 284 bathrooms, and parking space for 8,770 cars. 17,000 meals a day are served in its restaurants.

## Q **Why are horseshoes believed to be lucky?**

**A** *In 1700, Henri Misson, a Frenchman visiting Britain, asked villagers why they had horseshoes nailed above their doors. They said that it was to keep witches away. Horseshoes are made of iron and the strength of the iron was thought to protect from evil. Still today they are thought to bring good luck and many brides carry silver ones at their wedding. The position of the horseshoe is very important. It must point upwards like a cup so that the luck cannot fall out.*

## Q **Why do they drive on the left in Britain and on the right in other countries?**

**A** The reason for this goes back to the days when people travelled by horse. Most people are right-handed, and thus the left is the natural side to ride on if you are on horseback and need your right hand to hold a sword in case of trouble. So why didn't the rest of the world do the same? Because of Napoleon Bonaparte. He insisted that his armies marched on the right, and as he marched through Europe, he imposed this rule wherever he went. In the twentieth century Adolf Hitler did the same. Signs reading 'Rechts fahren' were put up whenever he took over a country.

The question suggests that only the British drive on the left, but in fact, out of 178 countries in the world, there are about 50 that drive on the left, including Japan. However, most of them are former British colonies.

## Q **How clever are dolphins?**

**A** Dolphins do have fairly large brains. There are many stories, ancient and modern, about dolphins saving sailors from drowning. Ever since the film *Flipper*, we have all seen how clever they are at learning how to do tricks. However, the truth is that dolphins are no more intelligent than rats, which can also be trained to do tricks. The stories about them rescuing people are true, but they automatically rescue anything which is about the same size as themselves. Sometimes they kill sharks and then immediately try to rescue them.

## Comprehension check

Work in groups.

1 Here are nine questions, one for each text.
   Which question goes with which text?
   What do the words underlined refer to?

a When was it built?
b What is a nice idea but not true?
c Do they rescue people because they are highly intelligent?
d Why is its position important?
e Why don't the majority of countries do this like the British?
f What is the most common explanation for this superstition?
g Why isn't it possible to provide an exact list of these?
h Where did the expression come from?
i Why are they more likely to have accidents?

   Now answer the questions a–i.

2 Find the following numbers in the texts. What do they refer to? Make a sentence about each number.

   4,000   40,000   50   200   1783
   1927   1700   17,000   82   76   16

## Producing a class poster

Work in small groups.

1 Make a list of some questions about the world that you would like to ask. Think of such things as places (countries, cities, buildings), people (famous people, languages, customs, superstitions), plants and animals, or things (machines, transport, etc.).

2 Check round the class to see if anyone can answer your questions.

3 Choose at least two questions and research the answers. You could go to an encyclopaedia. Write the answers in a similar style to the ones in the article.

4 Compile them into a poster for your classroom wall.

## ● LISTENING AND SPEAKING

## *The forgetful generation*

### Pre-listening task

You are going to listen to an item from a radio magazine programme called *Worldly Wise*. It is about the problem of forgetfulness in modern society.

1  **T.83a**  Read and listen to the introduction to the programme.

> 'Hello and welcome to *Worldly Wise*. How's your day been so far? Have you done all the things you planned? Kept all your appointments? Collected that parcel from the Post Office? Oh — and have you remembered to send your mother a birthday card? If so, well done! If not — you're not alone. Many of us are finding it more and more difficult to remember everything. Once upon a time we just blamed getting older for our absent-mindedness, but now experts are blaming our modern lifestyle. They say that we have become "the forgetful generation" and that day after day we try to do too much!'

2  Discuss the following in small groups.

– Does *your* lifestyle mean that you have a lot to remember to do each day? What kind of things fill your day?
– In what ways do you think modern society is busier and more stressful than a hundred years ago?
– In what ways do you help yourself remember all that you have to do each day? Or, have you got such a good memory that you don't have to do anything?

### Listening

1  **T.83b**  Listen to the stories of Ellen, Josh and Fiona, and take notes about them.

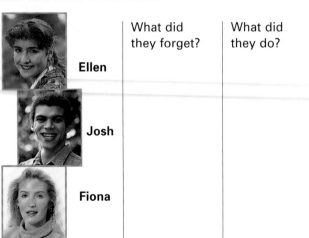

| | What did they forget? | What did they do? |
|---|---|---|
| **Ellen** | | |
| **Josh** | | |
| **Fiona** | | |

2  **T.83c**  Listen to the rest of the programme and answer the questions.

a  What is Professor Alan Buchan's job?
b  What is it about some modern day working practices that causes forgetfulness?
c  Why did the lady think that she was going mad?
d  In what ways was her lifestyle stressful?
e  What helped the lady feel more relaxed?
f  Does Professor Buchan advise using a personal computer to help remember things?
g  What does he advise? Why does he advise this?
h  How does the presenter try to be funny at the end of the interview?

### What do you think?

Have a class discussion.

Do you think Professor Buchan's explanation for forgetfulness is true?
Have you got any stories of forgetfulness, either your own or somebody else's?

## ● WRITING

### For and against

1  Do you live and/or work in a city? Is it very big? How many advantages and disadvantages of city life can you think of?
Write them down and compare them with a partner.

2  Read the text on the next page about the advantages and disadvantages of living in a city.

3  Answer the questions about the text.

a  There are three paragraphs. What is the purpose of each one?

b  Replace the words underlined with one of the following.

| | |
|---|---|
| in spite of | pros and cons |
| another point is that | one advantage is that |
| all things considered | for instance |
| to sum up | in my opinion |
| one disadvantage is that | especially |
| moreover | finally |

# Living in the City

● Living in a city has both advantages and disadvantages. On the plus side, it is often easier to find work, and there is usually a choice of public
5 transport, so you don't need to own a car. Also, there are a lot of interesting things to do and places to see. For example, you can eat in good restaurants, visit museums, and go to the theatre and to concerts. What is more, when you want to relax, you can usually find a park where you
10 can feed the ducks or just sit on a park bench and read a book. All in all, city life is full of bustle and variety and you need never feel bored.

● However, for every plus there is a minus. For one thing, you might have a job, but unless it is very well-paid, you
15 will not be able to afford many of the things that there are to do, because living in a city is often very expensive. It is particularly difficult to find good, cheap accommodation. What is more, public transport is sometimes crowded and dirty, particularly in the rush hour, and even the parks can
20 become very crowded, especially on Sundays when it seems that every city-dweller is looking for some open space and green grass. Last of all, despite all the crowds, it is still possible to feel very lonely in a city.

● In conclusion, I think that city life can be particularly
25 appealing to young people, who like the excitement of the city and don't mind the noise and pollution. However, many people, when they get older, and particularly when they have young children, often prefer the peace and fresh air of the countryside.

4  Write rough notes about the pros and cons of living in the country. Compare them with your partner.

5  Write three paragraphs called 'The Pros and Cons of Living in the Country'.
In the conclusion give your own opinion. Write about 250 words.

## PostScript

## Informal language

1  When we speak, we use a lot of informal language, depending on who we're speaking to!

Example
*These shoes cost ninety quid.*

In the dialogues, choose the informal words that fit best.

a  A  Let's have a break, shall we?
   B  All right. | I'm dying for a cuppa.
      I see.

b  A  My old man isn't at work today.
   B  Why? | What's he on about?
          | What's up with him?
   A  He was walking to work yesterday when this guy in a car knocked him over.
   B  Really! | Is he OK?
      Yuk!
   A  Well, | he was very lucky. He just got a few
      Right, | cuts and grazes.

c  A  Can I have one of your fags?
   B  Sure. | Help yourself. I've got loads.
      Damn.
   A  Oh! | Do *you* want one?
      Ta!
   B  No. I've just put one out.

d  A  Gimme your homework so I can copy it.
   B  What a pity! | You can do it yourself!
      No way!

e  A  Did you manage to fix the telly?
   B  Kind of. | The picture's OK, but the sound
      All right. | isn't quite right.
   A  What's on tonight?
   B  Dunno. Look in the paper.

f  A  What's that stuff called that you use to clean between your teeth?
   B  What do you mean?
   A  You see! | It's like string. White.
      You know!
   B  Oh! | You mean dental floss.
      Wow!
   A  That's it!

T.84  Listen and check your answers.

2  There are lots of other examples of informal language in the dialogues. How do we say them more formally? Be careful if you try to use them!

# 12

## Two weddings, a birth and a funeral!

Reported speech
Saying sorry

---

### Test your grammar

1 Read the story in a and write the actual words of the conversation in b.

The Marriage Proposal

a John greeted Moira and asked how she was. She told him she was fine and asked about him. He said he felt wonderful because they were together again. He added that it had been a long time since their holiday in Paris. She said she had loved every minute in Paris and that she would never forget it. She asked if they could go back there next spring. He said that he loved her. He asked if she would marry him and come to Paris with him for their honeymoon. She said that she would and that she loved him, too.

b John   'Hello, Moira. How _____?'
  Moira  'I'm _____.'
  John   'I feel _____ because
         we _____.
         It's been _____.'
  Moira  'I loved _____.
         I'll never _____.
         Can we _____?'
  John   'I _____.
         Will you _____?'
  Moira  'Oh yes, yes, I _____.'

2 Which is direct speech and which is reported speech?

3  T.85   Listen to the conversation. Are there any differences with yours?

## PRESENTATION (1)

### Reported statements and questions

1 Match a line in **A** with a line in **B** to make a natural sounding conversation. Put the letters a–j in the right box. Where is the conversation taking place? Who are Adam and Beatrice?

**A (Adam)**
a Are you on your own?
b How do you know John and Moira, then?
c Do you like big weddings?
d Where did you meet your husband, then?
e Why aren't you drinking?
f Have you travelled far to get here?
g Why aren't you wearing a hat?
h Where are you staying tonight?
i Can you give me a lift there?
j Yes, I am. Will there be enough room in your car?

**B (Beatrice)**
☐ I never wear hats.
☐ Oh, yes, lots. There won't be a problem.
☐ We're at the *Red Lion*.
☐ Because I'm driving.
☐ No, I'm not. I'm with my husband.
☐ I prefer smaller ones.
☐ Actually, I met him at a wedding.
☐ Yes, we have. We flew in from New York yesterday.
☐ I was at university with Moira.
☐ Yes, we can. Are you staying at the *Red Lion*, too?

2 **T.86a** Listen and check your answers.

3 Beatrice is telling her husband about the conversation with Adam. Read what she says.

'I've just met this really friendly young man. Do you know what he said to me?
First he asked me if I was on my own, and of course I said that I wasn't, I was with you.
Then he asked me how I knew John and Moira, and I told him I had been at university with Moira ...'

## ● Grammar questions

Read the sentences and answer the questions.

'***I'm*** *with my husband,' she said.*
*She said (that)* ***she was*** *with her husband.*

'***I was*** *at university with Moira,' she told him.*
*She told him (that)* ***she had been*** *at university with Moira.*

– What is the basic rule about the use of tenses in reported speech?
– What is the difference in the way *say* and *tell* are used?

'***Are*** *you on your own?' he asked.*
*He asked* ***if I was*** *on my own.*

'*How* ***do you know*** *John and Moira?' he asked.*
*He asked how* ***I knew*** *John and Moira.*

What differences are there between direct questions and indirect questions?
– When is *if* used?

## PRACTICE

## 1 Reporting a conversation

You are Beatrice. Continue reporting the conversation to a partner.

Example
*Then he asked if I liked ... and I said that I ...*

**T.86b** Listen and check your answer.

## 2 Grammar

1 Put the following direct speech into reported speech.

a 'I'm exhausted!' he said.
b 'Are you leaving on Friday?' she asked me.
c 'We haven't seen Jack for a long time,' they said.
d 'We flew to Madrid,' they said.

e 'Which airport did you fly from?' I asked them.
f 'The flight has been cancelled,' the announcement said.
g 'Our plane was delayed by five hours,' they told us.
h 'What time did it take off?' she asked.
i 'I'll help you unpack,' he said.
j 'I can't do this exercise,' he told the teacher.

2 What's the difference in meaning in the following examples of reported speech? Discuss with a partner.

a Beatrice said she lived in New York.
  Beatrice said she'd lived in New York.

b Moira told her mother that she'd love John.
  Moira told her mother that she loved John.

c Adam asked them how they'd travel to Paris.
  Adam asked them how they'd travelled to Paris.

What did the people actually say in direct speech?

## 3 Stress and intonation

1 Work in pairs and complete the conversation.
**A** is talking to **B** about a friend, George. **B** has not heard the same as **A**.

Example

a A He loves living in London.
  B But he told me _____ ! (hate)
b A He's moving to Canada.
  B But he told me _____ ! (Australia)
c A His girlfriend has left him.
  B But he told me _____ ! (he/leave/her)
d A He'll be thirty next week.
  B But he told me _____ ! (twenty-one)
e · A He went to Amsterdam for his last holiday.
  B But he told me _____ ! (Barbados)
f A He can't give up smoking.
  B But he told me _____ ! (three years ago)
g A He was given the sack last week.
  B But he told me _____ ! (promotion)
h A He's fallen in love with a French girl.
  B But he told me _____ ! (with me)

2 **T.87** Listen and check your answers. Pay particular attention to the stress and intonation.
Practise the dialogues with a partner.

# PRESENTATION (2)

## Reported commands

1  Read the newspaper article.

# 'A marriage made in hell!'

'We can get a good night's sleep now!' say Mr and Mrs Fish

**This is how Judge Margaret Pickles described the marriage of Patrick and Pauline**
5 **Peters as she ordered them to spend fourteen days in prison for rowing.**

THE COUPLE only married
10 six months ago and already they are famous for their rows. Neighbours complained that they could hear them shouting from the
15 bus stop six hundred yards away. Mrs Iris Fish, who lives opposite, said, 'First I asked them nicely to stop because my baby couldn't get to sleep,
20 but they didn't. Then my husband knocked at their door and told them to stop, but still they didn't. They threw a chair at him out of
25 the window. It just missed him! So that was it! We rang the police and asked them to come immediately.'

Mr and Mrs Peters
30 admitted they had been arguing. Mrs Peters said that she had accused Mr Peters of wasting their money on drink and gambling. However, they
35 denied throwing the chair.

The judge clearly did not believe them. She reminded them that they had already had two previous warnings
40 from the police and she told them that they would soon cool down in prison, especially as they would be in separate prisons. She advised
45 them to talk to a marriage guidance counsellor.

Mr and Mrs Fish and their baby are looking forward to some sleep! ■

2  Who is speaking? Find the lines in the text that report the following.
a  'You must go to prison for a fortnight.'
b  'It's terrible. We can hear them shouting from the bus stop.'
c  'Please, will you stop making that noise? My baby can't get to sleep.'
d  'Stop making that noise!'
e  'Please, can you come immediately?'
f  'OK. OK. It's true. We were arguing.'
g  'You've been wasting our money on drink and gambling again!'
h  'We didn't throw the chair.'
i  'Remember that you have already had two warnings from the police.'
j  'You'll soon cool down in prison.'
k  'I think you should see a marriage guidance counsellor.'

Compare the direct and reported speech.

## ● Grammar questions

– Four of the sentences a–k are commands or requests. Which are they? How are they reported in the text? Which verbs are used to report them?

– Underline the two sentences with *told* in the article. Which is a reported statement and which is a reported command?

– Which of the sentences below is a reported question? Which is a reported request?

  *I asked them to stop making a noise.*
  *She asked me if I knew the time.*

– *Say* and *tell* are both used to report statements. How many other reporting verbs can you find in the article?

# PRACTICE

## 1 Other reporting verbs

1 Which verb can be used to report the direct speech in the sentences below? Put a letter a – j in the box.

tell [c]    order [ ]    remind [ ]    beg [ ]    advise [ ]

ask [ ]    invite [ ]    warn [ ]    refuse [ ]    offer [ ]

a 'Please can you translate this sentence for me?' Maria said to Mark.
b 'Don't forget to send Aunt Maud a birthday card,' Mary said to her son.
c 'Sign on the dotted line,' the postman said to me.
d 'Please, please, please marry me. I can't live without you,' John said to Moira.
e 'Please come to our wedding,' John said to his boss.
f 'I'll pay for the next round,' Mark said.
g 'Don't run round the edge of the swimming pool or you'll fall in,' Mary said to her children.
h 'I won't go to bed!' Bobby said.
i 'You should talk to your solicitor,' Ben said to Bill.
j 'Take that chewing gum out of your mouth immediately!' the teacher said to Jo.

2 Change the sentences in Exercise 1 into indirect speech using the appropriate verbs.

## 2 Listening and speaking

You are policemen or policewomen taking statements.

1 Divide into two groups.

**Group A**

T.88a Listen to Pauline Peters and take notes about what she says happened.

**Group B**

T.88b Listen to Iris Fish and take notes about what she says happened.

2 Find a partner from the other group and report what you heard. Find the differences. Begin like this.

A *Pauline admitted that they sometimes argued. She said that …*
B *Iris complained that they argued every night. She said that …*

3 Write the reports for the police records.

# LANGUAGE REVIEW

## Reported statements

The usual rule for reported statements is that the verb form moves back one tense when the reporting verb is in the past tense.
The verbs *say* and *tell* are used to report statements but other verbs can also be used.

'He**'s having** a shower.'
*She said/told me (that) he **was having** a shower.*

'I**'ve lost** my wallet!'
*He said/complained (that) he **had lost** his wallet.*

'They **took** a taxi.'
*I said/thought (that) they **had taken** a taxi.*

'I**'ll ring you** tomorrow.'
*He said (that) he **would ring** me the next day./He promised to ring me the next day.*

The Past Simple and the Present Perfect both change to the Past Perfect.

## Reported questions

In reported questions the word order is like a statement. Verbs other than *ask* can be used.

When are you leaving?
*He asked (me)/He wondered **when I was leaving**.*

Where does John live?
*She inquired **where John lived**.*

Have you met Moira?
*He asked (me) **if I had met Moira**.*

When there is no question word, *if* is used, and there is no question mark.

## Reported commands

These are formed with the infinitive with *to*. The verbs *ask* and *tell* are used to report commands but other verbs can be used as well according to the meaning.

Sit down and be quiet!
*He told/ordered them **to sit** down and be quiet.*

Please can you give me a lift?
*She asked him **to give** her a lift.*

If I were you I'd see a doctor.
*She advised me **to see** a doctor.*

📖 Grammar Reference: page 140.

# VOCABULARY AND PRONUNCIATION

## Birth, marriage and death

1 Use your dictionary to sort the following words and phrases into the categories below.

| | | | |
|---|---|---|---|
| cot | bouquet | funeral | to get engaged |
| grave | pregnant | godmother | to have a baby |
| nappy | reception | cemetery | best man |
| grief | to bury | widow | maternity leave |
| wedding | bonnet | christening | bridegroom |
| pram | mourners | honeymoon | to get divorced |
| wreath | coffin | sympathy | to exchange rings |

| Birth | Marriage | Death |
|---|---|---|
| | | |
| | | |
| | | |
| | | |

2 Decipher the phonetic script to complete the puzzle. Find out the vertical word.

1 Three hundred people came to our /rɪˈsepʃn/ after the wedding.
2 I am my niece's /ˈɡɒdmʌðə/.
3 Thousands of /ˈmɔːnəz/ attended the king's funeral.
4 My sister is four months /ˈpreɡnənt/.
5 Our dog likes to /ˈberɪ/ his bone.
6 My daughter loves playing with her dolls' /præm/.
7 His brother was his /besˈmæn/.
8 The bridesmaid caught the /bʊˈkeɪ/.
9 In Britain you get eleven weeks' maternity /liːv/.
10 You haven't shown me very much /ˈsɪmpəθɪ/ for my toothache.
11 The Queen laid a /riːθ/ at the grave of the Unknown Soldier.
12 They say that old Bill died of /griːf/ after his wife died.
13 The emperor was buried in a gold /ˈkɒfɪn/.
14 Where did John and Liz go on their /ˈhʌnɪmuːn/?
15 The baby screamed throughout the /ˈkrɪsnɪŋ/.

3 What happens at births, weddings and funerals in your country?

# READING AND LISTENING

## *A birth and a death*

### Pre-reading task

Work in small groups.

1 Obviously you can't *remember* anything about the day you were born, but what have you been *told* about it? Who told you? What did they say?

Discuss what you have learnt with others in your group. Are there any interesting stories? Tell the whole class.

2 You are going to read an extract from Chapter one of *David Copperfield*, a very famous novel by the English writer, Charles Dickens.

– Do you know anything about the kind of novels Dickens wrote?
– Do you know any of their names?
– When did he write?
– What kind of people did he write about?

## Reading and listening (1)

## *A birth*

**T.89a**   Read and listen to Part I. It is the day of David Copperfield's birth and his young, widowed mother meets her dead husband's aunt, Betsey Trotwood.

What impression do you form of the characters of the two women? Have they met before?

# *David Copperfield*

CHAPTER 1

### I AM BORN (PART I)

I was born at Blunderstone, in Suffolk. I was a posthumous child. My father's eyes had closed upon the light of this world six months when mine opened on it.

5 On the afternoon of that eventful and important Friday, my mother was sitting by the fire, very timid and sad, and very doubtful of ever coming alive out of the trial that was before her, when, lifting her eyes to the window opposite, she saw a strange lady coming

10 up the garden. When she reached the house, instead of ringing the bell, she came and looked in at that window, pressing her nose against the glass. She gave my mother such a turn, that I have always been convinced I am indebted to Miss Betsey for having

15 been born on a Friday. Then she made a frown and a gesture to my mother, like one who was accustomed to being obeyed, to come and open the door. My mother went.

'Mrs David Copperfield, I *think*,' said Miss Betsey.

20 'Yes,' said my mother faintly.

'Miss Trotwood,' said the visitor. 'You have heard of me, I dare say?'

My mother answered that she had had the pleasure.

'Take off your cap, child,' said Miss Betsey, 'and let

25 me see you. Why, bless my heart! You are a very baby!'

My mother was, no doubt, unusually youthful in appearance; she hung her head, as if it was her fault, poor thing, and said sobbing, that indeed she was afraid she was but a childish widow, and would be a

30 childish mother *if* she lived.

'Well?' said Miss Betsey. 'And when do you expect?'

'I am all in a tremble,' faltered my mother. 'I don't know what's the matter. I shall die, I am sure!'

'No, no, no,' said Miss Betsey. 'Have some tea. I

35 have no doubt it will be a girl. I have a presentiment that it must be a girl. Now, child, from the moment of the birth of this girl …'

'Perhaps boy …,'

'Don't contradict. From the moment of this girl's

40 birth, child, I intend to be her friend. I intend to be her godmother, and I beg you'll call her Betsey Trotwood Copperfield. There must be no mistakes in life with *this* Betsey Trotwood. She must be well brought up. I must make that *my* care.'

## Comprehension check

Read the passage again and answer the questions. Use your dictionary to check new words.

1 Which of the following adjectives describe David's mother and which describe Betsey Trotwood? Which word describes neither of them?

    forceful   shy   confident   frightened   weak
    strong   miserable   impatient   bossy   meek
    insensitive   motherly   severe   flustered

2 Why was David a 'posthumous child'? (l.2) When had his father died? What was his father's name?
3 Why is that Friday called 'eventful and important'? (l.5)
4 What is 'the trial'? (l.8)
5 Why is David 'indebted to Miss Betsey for having been born on a Friday'? (l.14)
6 Why does Miss Betsey call David's mother 'child'? (l.24)
7 How many reasons can you find as to why David's mother is sad and frightened?
8 What is Betsey Trotwood absolutely certain about?

## What do you think?

1 What 'mistakes in life' might have happened to Miss Betsey Trotwood?

2 What do you think will happen next?

**T.89b** Read and listen to Part II. Who do you think Mr Chillip is?

### I AM BORN (PART II)

The mild Mr Chillip sidled into the parlour and said to my aunt in his meekest manner: 'Well, ma'am, I'm happy to congratulate you.'

'What upon?' said my aunt sharply.

5  Mr Chillip was flustered again by the extreme severity of my aunt's manner, so he made her a little bow and gave her a smile.

'Mercy on the man, what's he doing?' cried my aunt, impatiently. 'Can't he speak?'

10  'Be calm, my dear ma'am,' said Mr Chillip, in his softest accents. 'Be calm. I am happy to congratulate you. All is now over, ma'am, and well over.'

'How is she?' said my aunt, folding her arms.

'Well, ma'am, she will soon be quite comfortable,

15  I hope,' replied Mr Chillip. 'Quite as comfortable as we can expect a young mother to be. There cannot be any objection to your seeing her presently, ma'am. It may do her good.'

'And *she*. How is *she*?' said my aunt, sharply.

20  Mr Chillip laid his head a little more on one side, and looked at my aunt.

'The baby,' said my aunt. 'How is she?'

'Ma'am,' replied Mr Chillip, 'it's a boy.'

My aunt said never a word, but took her bonnet

25  by the strings, aimed a blow at Mr Chillip's head with it, put it on, and walked out. She vanished and never came back any more.

## Comprehension check

1 What is Betsey Trotwood's opinion of Mr Chillip? What does he think of her?
2 What is the misunderstanding between them?
3 Does Betsey go to see the baby?
4 What does Betsey Trotwood hit Mr Chillip with? Why does she hit him?
5 Why does she leave?

## What do you think?

– What do you think of Betsey Trotwood's behaviour?
– Do you think David Copperfield ever meets his aunt?

## Vocabulary

1 Find words in Part I that mean the same as the following.

shy   uncertain   was used to   hat   crying

2 Find words in Part II that mean the same as the following.

gentle   most humble   strictness   hat   hit   disappeared

## Language work

Read the account of Betsey Trotwood's conversation with David Copperfield's mother. Fill each gap with a suitable word from the box. Use each word once only.

> said   asked   begged   told (x 2)
> invited   expressed   suggested   added
> didn't answer   exclaimed   introduced

Miss Betsey Trotwood (1) _____ herself to David's mother, who (2) _____ that she had heard of her. Then Miss Betsey (3) _____ her to take off her cap so that she could see her properly. She was very surprised and (4) _____ that David's mother looked *very* young indeed! Next she (5) _____ when the baby was due, but David's poor mother (6) _____ the question, she just (7) _____ the fear that she would die having the baby. Miss Betsey dismissed these fears and (8) _____ her to have some tea. She (9) _____ that she had no doubt that the baby would be a girl. David's mother tentatively (10) _____ that it might be a boy but Miss Betsey (11) _____ her not to contradict, and (12) _____ her to call the baby Betsey Trotwood Copperfield.

## Reading and listening (2)

## *A death*

### Pre-reading task

1  **T.90**  Close your books and close your eyes. Listen to a poem by W H Auden (1907–1973). The poem is called *Funeral Blues*. Don't worry about understanding every word but try to understand the overall 'message'.
   It is a love poem.
   What has happened? How does the writer feel about the world now?

2  What words or lines can you remember? Share what you can remember with the rest of the class.

## Reading

Read the poem and answer the questions. Use your dictionary to check new words.

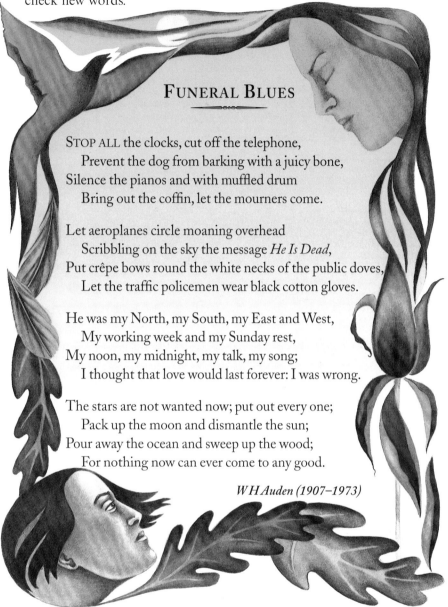

### FUNERAL BLUES

STOP ALL the clocks, cut off the telephone,
    Prevent the dog from barking with a juicy bone,
Silence the pianos and with muffled drum
    Bring out the coffin, let the mourners come.

Let aeroplanes circle moaning overhead
    Scribbling on the sky the message *He Is Dead*,
Put crêpe bows round the white necks of the public doves,
    Let the traffic policemen wear black cotton gloves.

He was my North, my South, my East and West,
    My working week and my Sunday rest,
My noon, my midnight, my talk, my song;
    I thought that love would last forever: I was wrong.

The stars are not wanted now; put out every one;
    Pack up the moon and dismantle the sun;
Pour away the ocean and sweep up the wood;
    For nothing now can ever come to any good.

*W H Auden (1907–1973)*

1  A loved one has died. What in general does the poet want the rest of the world to do? Why does the poet feel like this?
2  Which lines describe things that could possibly happen? Which describe impossible things?
3  Which verse describes the closeness of the relationship?
4  When you fall in love it is said that you see the world through 'rose-coloured spectacles'. What does this mean? In what ways is this poem the opposite of this?

## Learning by heart

1  Choose one verse and learn it by heart.

2  Recite the poem round the class.

## WRITING

### Correcting mistakes

1 Kati was a student of English in London, where she stayed with the Bennett family. She has now returned home. Read the letter she has written to Mr and Mrs Bennett. Her English has improved but there are still over 25 mistakes. How many can you find?

Szerens u. 43
Budapest 1125
Hungary
Friday 6 September

Dear Mr and Mrs Bennett

I am home now since two weeks, but I have to start work immediately, so this is the first time is possible for me to write. How are you all? Are you busy as usual? Does Andrew still work hard for his exam next month? I am miss you a lot and also all my friends from my English class. Yesterday I've received a letter from my greece friend, Christina, and she told about some of the other students. She say that Etsuko and Yukiko will write me from Japan. I am lucky because I made so many good friends during I was in England. It was really interesting for me to meet people from so many differents countries. I think that we not only improved our English (I hope this!) but we also knew people from all over the world and this is important.

My family are fine. They had a good summer hollyday by the lake. We are all very exciting because my brother will get married just before Christmas and we like very much his girlfriend. They have looked for a flat near the city centre but it is no easy to find one. If they won't find one soon they will have to stay here with us.

Please can you check something for me? I can't find my red scarf. I think maybe I have forgotten it in the cuboard in my bedroom.

Please write soon. My family send best wishes to you all. I hope I can come back next year. Stay with you was a very wonderful experience for me. Thank you for all things and excuse my mistakes. I already forget so much words.

Love

Kati

PS I hope you like the photo. It's nice, isn't it?

2 Compare the mistakes you have found with a partner. Correct the letter.

3 Write a thank-you letter to someone you have stayed with.

## Saying sorry

1 Read the conversations and put the correct expression from the box into the gap.

> (I'm) sorry   I *am* sorry   Pardon   Excuse me   What

a '_____, can you tell me where the post office is?'
 '_____, I'm a stranger here myself.'

b

'Ouch! That's my foot!'
'_____. I wasn't looking where I was going.'

c
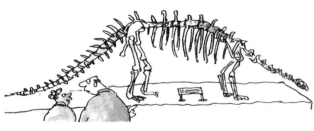

'_____, what's that creature called?'
'It's a Diplodocus.'
'_____?'
'A Diplodocus. D-I-P-L-O-D-O-C-U-S.'
'Thank you very much.'

d 'I failed my driving test for the sixth time!'
 '_____.'

e '_____! We need to get past. My little boy isn't feeling well.'

f 'Do you want your hearing aid, Grandma?'
 '_____?'
'I said: *Do you want your hearing aid?*'
 '_____?'
'DO YOU WANT YOUR HEARING AID?!'
'_____, I can't hear you. I need my hearing aid.'

2 **T.91a** Listen and check your answers. Act out the conversations, paying particular attention to stress and intonation.

3 What *exactly* would you say in the following situations? Respond in one or two sentences.

a You were cut off in the middle of an important phone call to a business colleague. You think there is a problem with the switchboard in your office. You ring your colleague back.

b You want the attention of the waiter in a very crowded restaurant. You want another large bottle of fizzy mineral water for your table.

c A friend tells you that she can't meet you for lunch as planned next Thursday because she suddenly has to go to an aunt's funeral.

d Your daughter, aged fourteen, tells you that she wants to go to an all-night party and take a bottle of your whisky with her.

e You thought you had bought a *medium* jumper, but when you get it home you see it's the wrong size. You take it back to the shop.

f You ask for directions in a foreign country, but you don't understand the reply. Ask the person to say it again.

g You want to get off a very crowded train at the next stop. You have a huge suitcase.

h Your dinner guest reminds you that he is vegetarian. You have just put a huge steak on his plate.

4 **T.91b** Listen to the sample answers. Were your answers similar?

# Tapescripts

## Tapescript 48

**I = Interviewer    N = Nancy Mann**

I   Who *do* you work for at the moment, Ms Mann?

N   Um, I work for the BBC World Service.

I   Ah, and how long *have* you worked for the BBC?

N   I*'ve* been with the BBC for five years. Yes, exactly five years.

I   And how long *have* you been their German correspondent?

N   For two years.

I   And what *did* you do before the BBC?

N   I worked as an interpreter for the EU.

I   As you know, this job is based in Geneva. *Have* you ever lived abroad before?

N   Oh yes, yes I *have*.

I   And when *did* you live abroad?

N   Well, in fact, I *was* born in Argentina and I lived there until I was eleven. Also, I lived and worked in Brussels for two years when I *was* working for the EU.

I   Mmm … That's interesting. *Have* you travelled much?

N   Oh yes, yes indeed. I*'ve* travelled all over western and eastern Europe, and I*'ve* also been to many parts of South America.

I   Mmm … And why *did* you go to these places?

N   Well, mostly for pleasure, but three years ago I went back to Argentina to cover various political stories in Buenos Aires for the BBC.

## Tapescript 49

a   She was born in Argentina in 1959.

b   She went to boarding school in England from 1970 to 1977.

c   She studied French and German when she was at Oxford University.

d   She hasn't spoken Spanish since she was in Buenos Aires three years ago.

e   She's worked in both eastern and western Europe at various times in her life.

f   She worked in Brussels for two years, from 1989 to 1991.

g   She's worked for the BBC for the last five years.

h   She hasn't worked abroad since her son was born four years ago.

i   She married for the first time when she was twenty-one.

j   She's been married three times.

k   She married for the third time last year.

## Tapescript 50a

### The news

a   The murderer Bruce Braden *has escaped* from Parkhurst Prison on the Isle of Wight.

b   After the heavy rain of the last few days, floods *have brought* chaos to drivers in the West Country.

c   Amy Carter, the kidnapped baby from Leeds, *has been found* safe and well in a car park in Manchester.

d   Two thousand car workers from a US car factory *have been made* redundant.

## Tapescript 50b

a   Last night, the murderer Bruce Braden *escaped* from Parkhurst Prison. Prison officers *found* his cell empty at six o'clock this morning.

b   Early this morning, floods *brought* chaos to many roads in Devon. Drivers left their cars and *walked* to work through the flood water.

c   Late last night, the kidnapped baby, Amy Carter, *was found* safe and well in a car park in the centre of Manchester. The car park attendant *heard* a noise coming from a rubbish bin and he *found* Amy wrapped in a warm blanket.

d   Two thousand car workers from the General Motors factory in Detroit *were made* redundant yesterday. The management *gave* them no warning. The men were shocked and furious when they *heard* the news yesterday evening.

## Tapescript 51

### Thomas Wilson – a retired man

**T = Thomas Wilson    P = Philippa**

P   How long have you been retired now, Grandpa?

T   Let me see. Er … it's four years. Yes, I've been retired nearly four years now. I suppose I'm used to it after all this time. But you know, I worked for *Courtaulds* for over forty years. Can you believe that? Forty years.

P   One job for forty years. Incredible! I remember when you retired and they gave you that gold watch. Do you like being retired? I'd get bored. I'm sure I would. Don't you get bored?

T   Well, I'm lucky. I've got my health so I can do a lot, I can get out a lot. I've just taken up golf, you know. It's a wonderful sport for an old man like me 'cos it's not really a sport at all, at least not the way your Grandpa plays it. It's just a good excuse for a walk, and I need an excuse since Rover died. I … I miss good old Rover; he and I were great friends … but I don't think I want another dog at my age. I go to the golf club twice a week. I've made some good friends there, you know. Have you met Ted and Marjorie? They're my age. Er … They're a lovely couple.

P   Er, no … I don't think I've met them, but didn't you go on holiday with them?

T   Yes, that's right. We went to Wales together last Easter. Oh … and we had a lovely time, a lovely time. I do appreciate company since your Grandma died … you know, I really miss your Grandma. Thirty-five years we were married, thirty-five years and still as much in love as the day we met. She was a wonderful lady, your Grandma.

P   Oh I know that, Grandpa. We all miss her so much. We all loved her so much.

T   So I like to keep busy. I've been on all sorts of special holidays, you know. Package holidays for senior citizens, and I …

P   Well, I know you went to visit Uncle Keith in Australia. *And* you've just come back from a cruise round the Caribbean. You're so brown.

T   I know. My word, that was an experience. I loved every minute of it! When you're older, I'll tell you about the American widow I met! … Miriam, she was called. Oh, just a baby of fifty-five, but she seemed to like me.

P   Grandpa!

T   And yes, of course, Keith. I saw him two years ago. You've not met your Australian cousins yet, have you? Oh, you'd love the baby, Kylie, she's beautiful. Looks just like your Grandma. But you know, I've also been to Spain and Morocco, *and* Turkey. These package holidays are so good for people like me.

P   Grandpa, next time, please think of me. Don't you want a companion? Can I come with you? I'd love a suntan like yours! We never go anywhere interesting.

T   Oh, Philippa, you know your mum and dad wouldn't let me. Not until you've finished your exams. Helen says I am a bad influence on you.

P   Well, I think *you* have more fun than *I* do! All I have to look forward to is exams and more exams and then years and years of work!

T   Oh Philippa. Don't wish your life away. Just enjoy it all. You only get one go at it!

## Tapescript 52

### On the telephone

a   Hello, this is Chesswood 285120. I'm afraid I'm not at home at the moment, but please leave your name and number after the tone and I'll get back to you as soon as I can. 'Hi, Annie. This is er … Pete here. Pete Nealy. Er … I need to speak to you about next weekend. Can you give me a ring? Erm … I'm at home, by the way. It's ten o'clock now and I'll be here all morning, er … at least until two o'clock. Yeah, thanks. Bye.'

b   'I'm afraid Mr Barrett's in a meeting. Can I take a message?'

'Yes, please. This is Pam Haddon. He rang me earlier and left a message on my answer phone and I'm returning his call. Can you tell him I'm back in my office now?'

c   'Shall I ask Miss Jackson to give you a call when she gets back?'
'Yes, please. I'm sure she's got my number but I'll give it to you again, just in case. It's 01924 561718.'

d   'Good morning. Payne and Stracey Advertising.'
'Good morning. Can I have extension 321, please?'

e   'Hello, Mrs Barrett … I'm afraid Mr Barrett's on another line at the moment. Do you want to hold or …? Oh, he's free now. I'm putting you through.'
'Thank you very much.'
'Hello …'
'Hello, Frank? It's me, Diana …'

f   'Hello. Is that Sandra?'
'No, I'm sorry, it isn't. She's just gone out. Can I take a message? She'll be back in a minute.'

# UNIT 8

## Tapescript 53a

**M = Mum   J = Jim**

M   Oh, dear! I hope everything will be all right. You've never been abroad before.
J   Don't worry, Mum. I'll be OK. I can look after myself. Anyway, I'll be with Anthony. We won't do anything stupid.
M   But what will you do if you run out of money?
J   We'll get a job of course!
M   Oh. What about if you get lost?
J   Mum! If we get lost, we'll ask someone the way, but we won't get lost because we know where we're going!
M   Oh. All right. But what if you can't read the directions?

## Tapescript 53b

M   But how will I know that you're all right?
J   When we get to a big city, I'll send you a postcard.
M   Oh. But Jim, it's such a long flight to Istanbul!
J   Mum! As soon as we arrive in Turkey, I'll give you a ring!
M   I'll be so worried until I hear from you.
J   It'll be OK, Mum. Honest!

## Tapescript 54

**J = Joe   S = Sue**

J   Goodbye, darling! Good luck with the interview!
S   Thanks. I'll need it. I hope the trains are running on time. If the trains are delayed, I'll get a taxi. If I'm late for the interview, I'll be furious with myself!
J   Just keep calm! Phone me when you can.

S   I will. As soon as I come out of the interview, I'll give you a ring.
J   When will you know if you've got the job?
S   They'll send me a letter in the next few days. If they offer me the job, I'll accept it, and if I accept it, we'll have to move house. You know that, don't you?
J   Sure. But we'll worry about that later.
S   OK. What are you doing today?
J   I can't remember. When I get to the office, I'll look in my diary. I don't think I'm doing much today.
S   Don't forget to pick up the children as soon as you get back from work.
J   I won't. You'd better go now. If you don't hurry, you'll miss the train.
S   OK. I'll see you this evening. Bye!
J   Bye, my love. Take care, and good luck!

## Tapescript 55

1   A   I'd go on a boat trip around the world.
    B   Oh, I wouldn't. I'd get so bored. I'd rather fly. It'd be so much quicker.
    A   No, I'd like to relax on the boat, sunbathe all day long, and have a waiter bring me a cold drink just when I want one. Ah, Heaven!
2   I wouldn't mind taking things easy for a bit, but then I'd like to just get on with my life, 'cos I'm very happy, really, with what I've got.
3   I'd buy all the toys in the world.
4   I would buy a field with the most beautiful view I could find, not very far away from where we live, if possible, and move my own house that I live in stone by stone and build it in that field.
5   I would first of all resign from my job as a teacher, and I would take the kids to Disneyland, and make sure they had the time of their life, and then I'd probably buy a property in Europe somewhere, just so we had the chance to go away for different holidays.
6   I would buy a football team.
7   Well, I wouldn't give up my job, because I've heard too many stories about people who go completely mad when they do that. I think I'd try to spend it all in a week or a month, and then I could forget all about it.
8   Erm … I would go ice-skating, go to the moon, on a rocket of course, and … go to the circus.

## Tapescript 56a

a   If Tony rings, tell him I'm at Andy's. He can get hold of me there.
b   If you've finished your work, you can have a break. But you must be back here in fifteen minutes.
c   If I'm not back by eight o'clock, don't wait for me. Go without me. I'll join you at the party.
d   If you've got the flu, you should go to bed. Keep warm and have plenty of fluids.
e   If you're ever in London, you must give me a ring. We could go out somewhere.
f   If you go to Australia, you have to have a visa. You can get one from the Embassy.

g   I'd buy a word processor if I could afford it. It would be really useful for work.
h   If I had more time, I might do an evening class. I'd love to be really good at photography.

## Tapescript 56b

1   What do you do if you can't get to sleep at night?
2   What will you do if the teacher gives us a lot of homework tonight?
3   What would you do if you saw someone stealing in a shop?
4   What will you do if the weather's good this weekend?
5   What would you do if you were in a place where smoking was forbidden, and someone started to light a cigarette?
6   What do you do if you're reading something in English and you come across a new word?
7   What would you do if you found a wallet with a lot of money and an address in it?
8   What do you do if you get a headache?
9   What would you do if you needed £1,000 very quickly?

## Tapescript 57

**Who wants to be a millionaire?**

Who wants to be a millionaire?
I don't.
Have flashy flunkies everywhere.
I don't.
Who wants the bother of a country estate?
A country estate is something I'd hate.

Who wants to wallow in champagne?
I don't.
Who wants a supersonic plane?
I don't.
Who wants a private landing field, too?
I don't.
And I don't 'cos all I want is you.

Who wants to be a millionaire?
I don't.
Who wants uranium to spare?
I don't.
Who wants to journey on a gigantic yacht?
Do I want a yacht? Oh, how I do not!

Who wants a fancy foreign car?
I don't.
Who wants to tire of caviar?
I don't.
Who wants a marble swimming pool, too?
I don't.
And I don't 'cos all I want is you.

## Tapescript 58

1   'I went to Alice's flat last night.'
'Oh, really! What was it like?'
'Well, it was absolutely wonderful.'
2   'When I got home, I told my parents that I'd failed the exams.'
'Oh, dear. What did they say?'
'Well, my mother was OK, but my father, he went mad!'

3 'We went out for a meal last night.'
  'Where did you go?'
  'That new restaurant near the station.'
  'What was the food like?'
4 'We had a great time skiing in Switzerland.'
  'Where did you go?'
  'Zermatt.'
  'Was the weather good?'
  '…'
5 'It took hours to get here.'
  'Why?'
  'The traffic! It was incredible!'

## Tapescript 59

**1 Amnesty International**

Amnesty International is a world-wide organization, independent of any government or political party. It is our aim to release prisoners of conscience. These are men and women who are in prison not because they have broken the law, but because of their beliefs, colour, language, or religion. We try to get fair and early trials by publicizing their cases and by putting pressure on their governments to practise basic human rights.

Amnesty International has been in operation for over twenty years, and in that time we have helped prisoners in over sixty countries. We have won several peace prizes, including the Nobel Peace Prize in 1978.

Each year we handle, on average, nearly 5,000 individual cases. Please help us. We need your donations to make us unnecessary in this world.

**2 The RSPCA**

Founded in 1824, the RSPCA is the world's oldest animal welfare organization. We work to promote kindness and to prevent cruelty to animals within all lawful means throughout England and Wales. Every year we find new homes for about 80,000 animals, we treat over 200,000 sick animals ranging from hedgehogs to horses, and we investigate over 100,000 complaints of cruelty.

We also work for the welfare of animals in the wild, such as whales and badgers. We are the world experts at cleaning and rehabilitating birds that have been damaged in oil spills. Every year nearly 3 million animals are used in research laboratories, and we oppose all experiments that cause pain and suffering.

We work with both governments and the farming industry to promote humane methods in the rearing of farm animals. Intensive farming methods can cause many animal welfare problems.

The society is a charity, and receives no aid from the government. Our running costs amount to £38 million a year. Please give generously.

**3 Drought and Famine in Africa**

Drought and famine have come to Africa again this year, just as they have every year for the past fifteen years. In some parts of Africa it hasn't rained for three years. There have been no crops, and the animals on which many people depend died long ago. Refugees are pouring from the countryside into the towns in their desperate search for food, and it has been estimated that over a thousand people are dying every day.

We are supplying towns and camps with food and medical supplies, but our efforts are drops in the ocean. We need a hundred times more food and medical supplies, as well as doctors, nurses, blankets, tents, and clothes. Your help is needed now before it is too late. Please give all you can. No pound or penny will ever be better spent or more appreciated.

## Tapescript 60

### Maggie and Anna

**M = Maggie   A = Anna**

M  I'm bored!
A  Well, it's a lovely day. Why don't we take the dog for a walk?
M  No, I don't feel like going for a walk. I'm too tired.
A  You need to get out! Let's go shopping!
M  Oh, no! I couldn't bear it! I'd rather do anything but that!
A  OK, then. Shall we watch the telly?
M  That's a good idea!
A  Do you want the news on ITV?
M  Mmm, I'd rather watch *Neighbours* on BBC1. It's just started.

### Paul and Billy

**P = Paul   B = Billy**

P  I'm broke, and I don't get paid for two weeks! What am I going to do?
B  If I were you, I'd get a job that paid more money.
P  Oh, why didn't I think of that? Thanks, Billy. It doesn't help me now, does it?
B  Well, then, you'd better get a loan from the bank.
P  No, I couldn't do that. I owe them too much already.
B  Why don't you ask your parents? They'd help you.
P  No, I'd rather not. I'd rather sort out my problems on my own.
B  Then you ought to ask your boss for a pay rise.
P  Good idea, but I've already tried that and it didn't work.
B  Oh. Well, I suppose I could lend you some.
P  Really? That would be great! Thanks Billy. You're a real mate. I'll pay it back, honest!

# UNIT 9

## Tapescript 61

a  'Mr and Mrs Brown never go on holiday.'
   'They can't have much money.'
b  'The phone's ringing!'
   'It might be Jane.'
c  'Paul's taking his umbrella.'
   'It must be raining.'

d  'There are three fire engines!'
   'There must be a fire somewhere!'
e  'I don't know where Hannah is.'
   'She could be in her bedroom.'
f  'My aunt isn't in the kitchen.'
   'She can't be cooking dinner.'
g  'Whose coat is this?'
   'It might be John's.'
h  'We've won the lottery!'
   'You must be joking.'

## Tapescript 62

a  A  A half of lager and a fizzy mineral water, please.
     B  Ice and lemon with the water?
     A  Yes, please. And do you do bar meals?
     B  Yes, we do.

b  I don't work regular hours and I like that. I'd hate one of those nine to five office jobs. Also, I meet a lot of really interesting people. Of course, every now and then there's a difficult customer, but most times people are really nice. I took that really famous film star to the airport last week, now what was her name? Er … you know, she's in that film – er, what's it called? Anyway she was really nice. Gave me a big tip!

c  A  So how did you get on?
     B  Oh it was good? They're very nice actually.
     A  Were you nervous?
     B  Yeah, a bit. Michael really wanted them to like me. I think they did. They were very kind anyway.
     A  And did you tell them that you and Michael are going to get married?
     B  No, next time. I just wanted to get to know them first.

d  A  We've never had one before.
     B  Really? We've always had them in our family. We're all mad about them.
     A  Well, we are now. The kids love her. And she is so good with them, ever so good-natured. But it wasn't fair to have one when we lived in town.
     B  It's OK if they're small and you live near a park, but I know what you mean. What's she called?
     A  Trudy.

e  A  Pull! Pull! Not too quickly!
     B  I can't. It's really strong.
     A  Come on. In then out. You're doing fine. Careful!
     B  Yaow!
     A  The one that got away!

## Tapescript 63a    See page 88

## Tapescript 63b

**A = Andy   C = Carl**

A  Hi! Carl? It's Andy.
C  Andy!
A  Yeah. How are you? Feeling better?
C  No! Not a lot. I have to sit down most of the time. It's too tiring – walking with a crutch.
A  Really? Still using a crutch, eh? So you're not back at work yet?

C No. And I'm bored to death. I don't go back to the hospital for two more weeks.

A Two more weeks! That's when the plaster comes off, is it?

C Well, I hope so. I can't wait to have two legs again! Anyway. How are you? Still missing all that snow and sun?

A No, I'm fine. The suntan's fading though. Josie's is too. She sends love, by the way.

C Love to her, too. I miss you all. By the way, have you got any holiday photos back yet?

A Yes, yes, I have. I got them back today. They're good. I didn't realize we'd taken so many.

C What about that one you took of that amazing sunset behind the hotel?

A Yes, the sunset. It's a good one. All of us together on Bob and Marcia's balcony, with the mountains and the snow in the background. It's beautiful. Brings back memories, doesn't it?

C Yeah. The memory of me skiing into a tree!

A Yes, I know. I'm sorry. At least it was towards the end; it could have been the first day. You only came home two days early.

C OK, OK. Oh, Andy, have you written to the tour operator yet to complain about that car we hired? They promised us a bigger one.

A Yes, we have. Yesterday, in fact. Bob wrote it and we all signed it. I don't know if it'll do any good, but it's worth a try.

C And Marcia's suitcase, did that turn up?

A Yeah. They found it. It arrived on the next flight. Marcia was delighted.

C I'll bet she was! I suppose it was a good two weeks really, wasn't it?

A Sure. Some ups and downs, but generally I think we all got on well and had a great time. Shall we go again next year?

C Well, I'd like to. All six of us again. Julie wants to, too. She fell in love with Switzerland, but she says she'll only come if I don't break a leg!

A Good! Great! It's a date. Next time, look out for the trees! I'll ring again soon, Carl. Take care!

# Tapescript 64

a 'John didn't come to school yesterday.'
  'He must have been ill.'

b 'Look at my new gold watch!'
  'Wow! You can't have bought it yourself.'

c 'Why is Isabel late for class?'
  'Um … She might have overslept.'

d 'I can't find my homework.'
  'You must have forgotten it.'

e 'The teacher's checking Maria's work.'
  'She can't have finished already!'

f 'Did you know that Charles got top marks in the exam?'
  'He must have cheated!'

g 'Where's my umbrella?'
  'Oh! You could have left it on the train.'

# Tapescript 65

## Brothers and sisters

**1 A large family**

**J = Jillie   I = Interviewer**

J I'm the youngest of nine children. My eldest sister is still alive, age ninety-three and there are sixteen years between us. We were four girls, four boys, and then me.

I And how well did you all get on together when you were children?

J Really, amazingly well. Being the youngest, I and my two young brothers rather looked on the rest of the family as 'the others', 'cos by that time they were either away at school or working. But we were always fond of one another and now of course, the roles have rather reversed because they were inclined to keep an eye on us and now — we younger ones, the two youngest, are very busy looking after the remainder, 'the ancient ones'.

I Tell me how your relationship with your sister, Joy, has changed over the years.

J Joy was the sister who used to … in her holidays … used to take me off er … for lovely walks and teach me a great deal about the countryside. And she eventually became a nun and disappeared to Australia for twenty-three years. And we wrote to one another and I was still her little sister. When she came back, shortly after my husband died and the whole relationship changed enormously, and we became tremendous friends, we've never looked back.

I What do you see as the main advantage and disadvantage of coming from such a large family?

J I think the main advantage was this marvellous example of our parents, of how to enjoy life on a shoestring, because we were very much the poor relations, and it always amused us that our wealthy young cousins envied us so much. We had the old bikes and all the freedom in the world, and they were stuffed into Eton suits and expected to behave themselves.

I Disadvantages?

J I think it was very tough at a certain stage to have hand-me-down clothes, especially for a vain little girl, and not to have much in the way of parties and perhaps not to be able to go abroad, as other children did. But the advantages outweighed the disadvantages enormously, there's no doubt about that.

I Six out of the nine of you are still alive. How closely have you kept in touch over the years?

J Very closely. For many years now we've had an annual family party for three generations. And the touching thing is that the two younger generations just love to come, and there are anything up to sort of thirty-five of us meet up, once a year, in one or other of the houses, and have this marvellous lunch and tea-party, and lots of photographs are taken. And we've now got

baby twins that were handed round this time. D'you know, and all this sort of thing … marvellous!

**2 An only child**

**P = Philippa   I = Interviewer**

P I'm an only child and basically I think the disadvantages far outweigh the advantages of being an only child. I was erm … relatively happy as a young child but as you get older, I think being an only child gets more difficult to deal with.

I When you were little it wasn't too bad being an only child?

P No, but I was very lucky; I had lots of cousins. I had fourteen first cousins and most of them lived in the same town that I grew up in until I was ten, so we all played together and what have you. And I had a friend who lived next door to me, who was my best friend, who was the same age as me and so she was a bit like a sister then I suppose, and it wasn't until we moved away from there that I think it became more difficult being an only child.

I You said to me once that it was when you were a teenager that it was particularly hard. Why was that?

P Yes. I think … I think when you're a teenager, you're quite unsure of how to deal with things, especially your parents anyway, and when you're on your own, you have nobody to compare notes with or to sort of say, are my parents being unreasonable or not, you just have to work it out for yourself, and that I think is quite hard really.

I Some people who come from large families might envy you because you had all of your parents' attention.

P Yes. That of course has its negatives as well as its positives, doesn't it? I think. You have all of their attention but you don't always want it, especially as a teenager. I think at that point in your late teens, you want to move away from your family a little bit, and … and sort of explore other relationships, and if you have all of your parents' attention, you can't necessarily do that very well.

I What about now that you're an adult? Does the fact of being an only child have any impact on your life at all?

P Er … yes. I think it's probably again quite difficult really. Erm … my father died about ten years ago, so of course I'm the one who's left totally responsible for my mother. I'm the one that has to look after her if she has a problem, and help her if she needs help in any way. There's nobody else to help at all. So yes, I think it does have problems then, too.

I You have two children of your own. Was that a conscious decision because you decided that you didn't want one of your children to be an only child?

P Yes, very definitely. Yes, yes, I didn't want that to happen and I feel sorry for other children who are only children. I must say, I think that's ... at this age at the age of my children, it's probably fine but as they get older, I think it gets more difficult.

I  So all in all, being an only child is not something you'd recommend.

P  No, certainly not, no, no.

## Tapescript 66a–d    See pages 92–93

## Tapescript 67

### Polly and her friends

**P = Polly    A–J = Polly's friends**

A  I want to travel the world.
P  So do I.
B  I don't want to have lots of children.
P  Neither do I.
C  I can speak four languages.
P  I can't.
D  I can't drive.
P  Neither can I.
E  I'm not going to marry until I'm 35.
P  Neither am I.
F  I went to America last year.
P  So did I.
G  I have never been to Australia.
P  I have.
H  I don't like politicians.
P  Neither do I.
I  I am bored with the British Royal family.
P  So am I.
J  I love going to parties.
P  I don't.

# UNIT 10

## Tapescript 68    See pages 96–97

## Tapescript 69

a  How long has he been learning to drive?
b  How many lessons has he had?
c  How much has he spent on tuition?
d  How many instructors has he had?
e  How many times has he crashed?
f  How long has he been praying for a driving-licence?
g  What have his instructors been telling him?
h  How many times has he taken his test?
i  How has he been celebrating?

## Tapescript 70

A  *Can you* drive?
B  Oh, yes.
A  *How long have you been driving?*
B  Since I was seventeen. About ten years.
A  *Have you got* a car?
B  Yes, I have. It's a Renault.
A  How long *have you had* it?
B  About a year.
A  How much *did you* pay *for it?*
B  Well, I got it second-hand, and I think I paid about six thousand pounds.
A  How many kilometres *has it done?*
B  Ooph! I'm not sure.

A  About how many?
B  About forty thousand kilometres, I'd say.
A  *Have you* ever *had an accident?*
B  Not in this car, no, but I had one in the car I had before.
A  What happened?
B  Well, the roads were wet because it had been raining, and I skidded into another car.
A  Whose fault *was it?*
B  Oh, it was my fault. I was going too fast.

## Tapescript 71

A  You look tired! What have you been doing?
B  I've been getting ready to go on holiday.
A  Have you done everything?
B  Well, I've packed the cases and I've been to the bank, but I haven't booked the taxi yet.

## Tapescript 72

a  A  When was she born?
   B  In 1950.
b  A  When was her collection of poems published?
   B  In April 1958, when she was just eight years old.
c  A  When did her mother die?
   B  On 16 September 1961.
d  A  When did she get married for the first time?
   B  While she was still at university – in spring 1970.
e  A  When did she graduate?
   B  On 20 June 1971.
f  A  When was her daughter born?
   B  On 14 June 1972.
g  A  When did she go to India and the Far East?
   B  After her divorce. She was twenty-nine at the time.
h  A  When did she get married for the second time?
   B  At 10.30 on 3 August 1988.
i  A  How long did her first marriage last?
   B  Nine years.
j  A  How long has she been living in Paris?
   B  Since 1988.

## Tapescript 73

**I = Interviewer    J = Joanna**

1  I  How long are you in the States for?
   J  Two weeks.
2  I  How long have you been in the States?
   J  Eight days.
3  I  When do you go back to England?
   J  At the end of the week, in five days' time.
4  I  Where were you the day before yesterday?
   J  I was in Chicago.
5  I  Where were you this time last week?
   J  Er, I was in New York.
6  I  Where will you be the day after tomorrow?
   J  I'll be in Denver.

## Tapescript 74

driving-licence    chain smoker    postbox
driving test    business partner    postman
wallpaper    ashtray    postcode
press conference    postcard    post
   office

## Tapescript 75a

**I = Interviewer    M = Margaret Tyler**

I  Margaret, may I ask you what you do for a living?
M  Well, I work for a children's charity. That's a full-time job, but I also have guests coming to stay with me at weekends.
I  You mean ... paying guests?
M  Yes. This house, which is called Heritage House, is a bed-and-breakfast place, too.
I  What I can see around me, Margaret, is amazing! How long have you been collecting all this royal memorabilia?
M  Well, I first got interested in the Royal family when I saw the wedding of Princess Margaret on TV in 1960. Um, my father wouldn't let us have a television in the house because he said it would stop me doing my homework, so on the day of the wedding, I went round to a friend's house, and I just sat in front of the screen, mesmerized. But it wasn't until later that I started collecting. I've been collecting for eighteen years. The first things I bought were a dish with the Queen's head in the centre, and a few Coronation mugs to go with it.
I  What sort of things have you got?
M  Oh, everything! Oh, pictures, paintings, ashtrays, hundreds of mugs, um ..., er ... tea-pots, tea-cloths, biscuit tins, posters, books, flags, toast racks, egg cups, candle sticks, the lot! I've got over four thousand Royal souvenirs.
I  All in this house?
M  All in this house, yes. The house has been extended three times to fit it all in. They're in all the rooms downstairs, and in the four bedrooms upstairs, and in the attic, too.
I  Incredible!
M  It takes all my spare time to keep everything clean and dusted. I'm always playing around, making a special area for one of the Royals or another. Er ... It keeps me amused for hours, and the visitors who come, mainly foreign visitors, never get tired of talking about our Royal family.
I  Is there one piece that's your favourite?
M  Yes, I was desperately upset when Princess Diana and Prince Charles split up, and I wrote to Princess Diana, saying I hoped they might get together again. I got a lovely letter back from her Lady-in-Waiting, Sarah Campden, and that's the most important part of my whole collection.
I  Have you had to spend a lot of money on your collection?
M  Oh, I don't know. I've never thought about it. No, I don't think so. Once, when Prince Andrew married Fergie, a shop filled its

windows with nothing else but mementoes of them, and I walked in and bought the lot. But I … I can't remember how much it was.

I   And where do you get it all from?

M   All over the place. There are lots of people who collect this stuff. I go up and down the country. We have conventions where we swap things. And there are specialist magazines and shops, and … and jumble sales.

I   Have you ever had to fight to get something you really wanted?

M   Well, once I was in a shop and the shop keeper was drinking his tea from a lovely Coronation mug. I offered to buy it from him but he wasn't interested. So off I went to a shop nearby and bought a plain mug and presented it to him. 'Now will you do a swap?' I said to him. And he did. Oh, it was driving me mad, the thought of him using this mug every day! I wanted to give it a proper home!

I   Is there anything you haven't got that you'd really like to have?

M   Not a thing, but a person. Princess Diana is my favourite Royal. She's warm, wonderful, giggly, real. I'd love to meet her.

I   Well, I hope your dream comes true! If she ever came to your house, she'd feel very at home!

## Tapescript 75b

**I = Interviewer    T = Ted Hewitt**

I   Ted, we're sitting in your dining-room, surrounded by a wonderful collection of miniature coaches. When did you start collecting them?

T   Well, some of them date back to when I was a child, and they were given to me as toys, so … at the age of five or six. But the bulk of them I've added er … in the last ten, fifteen years.

I   Now, I can understand a child enjoying playing with them, but why did you carry on, and actually make this collection?

T   Well, it's because of my family background, erm … I'm the third generation in a family coach business, so I've been … lived with and been brought up with coaches all my life.

I   Mmm. So you've got the real thing, and … and the miniatures as well?

T   That's right, yes.

I   How many miniatures do you think you've got?

T   I haven't counted them for a long time, but there must be at least five hundred, I should think.

I   Which is your favourite?

T   Well, my favourite is probably what is also the oldest, and that's a er … little tin-plate double-decker bus, loosely based on a London Transport double-decker of the period.

I   And how old is that?

T   Er … that would have been manufactured in the … in the late thirties, early forties …

I   And …

T   … I think.

I   And we've got it here. It's lovely. And it …

and it … it … it winds up. Will you … will you …?

T   Yes. It's …

I   … do it for us?

T   It's a clockwork. So, er … winds up like that.

I   Oh, it's marvellous. How long have you had that? Did you have it as a child?

T   Er … no, no. That one doesn't date from that period. Erm … probably about ten years I've had that one.

I   Hmm. Do you keep your collection all in here? Is this the complete collection?

T   The bulk of it is here, but er … I have others in other rooms of the house, and some stored up in the attic, as well.

I   Do many people collect miniature coaches? Where … where do you get your coaches from? Where do you find them?

T   Yes, there are a surprisingly huge number of people collect buses and coaches, and erm … there are specialist shops that sell them. And then there's also a … a network of what are called swapmeets, where people go and trade in either current models or old models. So there's no difficulty in finding … models at all.

I   Are they expensive? If I decided that I wanted to collect …?

T   No, not necessarily. You can … you can buy contemporary models … anything from about two ninety-nine upwards. And the sky's the limit.

I   Give me a figure.

T   Oh, some people pay thousands and thousands for a specific model.

I   Which do you think was your most expensive?

T   I don't really know. Erm … I've never paid more than … probably about fifty, sixty pounds. I think, yes.

I   Have you got any very rare ones that people would fight for?

T   I've got some that have … have become rare. Weren't particularly rare when … when I bought it. It's … there's no rhyme or reason, but there … there is one that I bought probably for seven or eight pounds which is now worth about a hundred and eighty. And that's quite good in … sort of seven or eight years. That's not bad.

I   Would you ever … would you ever sell it?

T   No, I don't think so. Unless I had to. No.

I   No.

T   No. I'm too attached to them to sell them. It's like the real ones.

I   Are there any that you would really like to have that you haven't got, that you … you look for when you go to these swapmeets?

T   There's a lot that I'm tempted by, but er … no, no one specific model erm … financial constraint is the … is the problem, I'm afraid. However, if a model appears of an actual vehicle that I … that I own, then financial constraint or not … no, I would have to have it, I think.

I   Well, I think they're all lovely. Thank you very much, Ted.

T   Thank you.

# UNIT 11

## Tapescript 76   See page 107

## Tapescript 77

**A = Clerk in the tourist office   R = Rosie**

A   Good afternoon.

R   Hello. I wonder if you could help me. I've just arrived here, and I'm looking for somewhere to stay.

A   Uh huh.

R   Can you tell me where I can find a cheap hotel?

A   Certainly. There are a few around here, but the nearest and one of the nicest is just around the corner. It's called the Euro Hotel. Would you like me to phone to see if they have a room?

R   No, that's OK. I'll just wander round there myself. Ah! Another thing. I need to change some travellers' cheques, but I don't know what time the banks close.

A   They close at 7 o'clock in the evening.

R   Right, thanks. This is a very pretty town, isn't it? It looks terribly old. Have you any idea how old this town is?

A   Yes, it was founded in the thirteenth century.

R   Really? As old as that? Wow! Well, I'd better get going. Oh, I'm not sure if we're near the centre of town, because I've only just arrived.

A   Yes, this square out here is just about the centre.

R   Thanks very much. Thanks for your help. I'll go to … oh, sorry, I can't remember which hotel you suggested.

A   The Euro Hotel.

R   The Euro. Thanks a lot. Bye.

## Tapescript 78

**The news**

There's been a train crash in the north of the country, and there are fears that up to five people have been killed. It happened at XXXX o'clock this morning. The train was going from London to XXXX.

Lucie Courtney, the six-year-old girl from XXXX who went missing from her home last Thursday, has been found safe and well. She was found by XXXX. She'd gone to stay with her grandparents.

There's been a robbery at a bank in Manchester. About XXXX men dressed as policemen went into the bank and stole XXXX pounds. They escaped in a XXXX.

And finally sport. Liverpool played Real Madrid in the European Cup last night. It was a closely fought match, and the final score was XXXX.

And in boxing, Louis Henderson is the new heavyweight champion. He beat XXXX in Las Vegas last night. He said after the fight XXXX. And that's the end of the news.

## Tapescript 79   See page 109

## Tapescript 80

**C = Caroline Bailey   N = Norma, her secretary**

C  Now, what's happening today? I've got a meeting this afternoon, *haven't I*?

N  Yes, that's right. With Henry and Ted.

C  And the meeting's here, *isn't it*?

N  No, it isn't. It's in Ted's office, at 3.00.

C  Oh! I'm not having lunch with anyone, *am I*?

N  No, you're free all morning.

C  Phew! I'll start on that report, then. Er ... I signed all my letters, *didn't I*?

N  No, you didn't, actually. They're on your desk, waiting for you.

C  Ah, right! And er ... tomorrow I'm going to Scotland, *aren't I*?

N  Yes. You're booked on the early morning shuttle.

C  OK. It doesn't leave until 8.00, *does it*?

N  8.15, to be precise.

C  Gosh, Norma! Where would I be without you?

## Tapescript 81a

**R = question tag rises;  F = question tag falls**

a  It isn't very warm today, *is it*? (F)

b  The weather forecast was wrong again, *wasn't it*? (F)

c  You can cook, *can't you*? (R)

d  You don't eat snails, *do you*? (R)

e  You've got a CD, *haven't you*? (R)

f  Sally's very clever, *isn't she*? (F)

g  There are a lot of people here, *aren't there*? (F)

h  The film wasn't very good, *was it*? (F)

i  I am a silly person, *aren't I*? (F)

j  You aren't going out dressed like that, *are you*? (R)

## Tapescript 81b

a  'It isn't very warm today, is it?' (F)
   'No, it's freezing.'

b  'The weather forecast was wrong again, wasn't it?' (F)
   'Yes! It always is, though, isn't it?'

c  'You can cook, can't you?' (R)
   'Me? No! I can't even boil an egg.'

d  'You don't eat snails, do you?' (R)
   'Yuk! No, I don't! They're disgusting!'

e  'You've got a CD, haven't you?' (R)
   'Believe it or not, I haven't. I've got a tape recorder, though.'

f  'Sally's very clever, isn't she?' (F)
   'Yes. She's as bright as a button.'

g  'There are a lot of people here, aren't there?' (F)
   'I know! It's absolutely packed! I can't move!'

h  'The film wasn't very good, was it?' (F)
   'Terrible! The worst I've seen for ages.'

i  'I am a silly person, aren't I?' (F)
   'No, you're not. Just because you made one mistake doesn't mean you're silly.'

j  'You aren't going out dressed like that, are you?' (R)
   'Why? What's wrong with it? I thought I looked really smart.'

## Tapescript 82

1  A  You broke that vase, didn't you?
   B  Yes, I did. I dropped it. I'm sorry.
   A  You'll buy another one, won't you?
   B  Yes, of course. How much was it?
   A  £200.
   B  It *wasn't* £200, was it?!
   A  Yes, it *was*.

2  A  It's so romantic, isn't it?
   B  What is?
   A  Well, they're really in love, aren't they?
   B  Who are?
   A  Paul and Mary.
   B  Paul and Mary *aren't* in love, are they?!
   A  Oh, yes, they are. They're mad about each other.

3  A  Have you paid the electricity bill?
   B  No, *You've* paid it, haven't you?
   A  No, I haven't!
   B  But you *always* pay it, don't you?
   A  No, I don't. *I* always pay the telephone bill.
   B  Oh, yes. Sorry.

4  A  We love each other, don't we?
   B  Er ... I think so.
   A  We don't ever want to part, do we?
   B  Well ...
   A  We'll get married and have six children, won't we?
   B  What!? You haven't bought me a ring, have you?
   A  Yes, I have. Diamonds are forever.
   B  Oh, dear!

5  A  Helen didn't win the lottery, did she!?
   B  Oh, yes, she did. She won £2,000,000!
   A  She isn't going to give it all away, is she?
   B  Oh, yes, she is.
   A  She's very kind. Not many people would do that, would they?
   B  Well, *you* certainly wouldn't, would you?

6  A  That *isn't* a letter from Bertie, is it?
   B  Yes, it is. He hasn't written for six months, has he?
   A  What does he want?
   B  He wants to borrow some money, doesn't he?
   A  I'm not lending him another penny!
   B  You've already lent him £2,000, haven't you?
   A  I certainly have.

7  A  You *haven't* forgotten the map, have you?
   B  Oh, dear. Yes, I have.
   A  But I put it next to your rucksack.
   B  I didn't see it, did I?
   A  So, how can we find the village?
   B  We could ask a policeman, couldn't we?
   A  There *aren't* many policemen on this mountain.

8  A  We can't afford that new car, can we?
   B  Are you sure? Haven't we saved a lot of money?
   A  Yes, but, we need that money, don't we?
   B  What for?
   A  Our old age.
   B  You're joking, aren't you?
   A  Yes, I am. I've just bought it for you!
   B  Wow!

## Tapescript 83a

**The Forgetful Generation**

**Presenter**

Hello and welcome to Worldly Wise. How's your day been so far? Have you done all the things you planned? Kept all your appointments? Collected that parcel from the Post Office? Oh – and have you remembered to send your mother a birthday card? If so, well done! If not – you're not alone. Many of us are finding it more and more difficult to remember everything. Once upon a time we all just blamed getting older for our absent-mindedness, but now experts are blaming our modern lifestyle. They say that we've become 'the forgetful generation' and that day after day we try to do too much!

## Tapescript 83b

**Ellen**

Last year I finished university and I got a job in the same town, Canterbury, where I was at university. And one day, for some reason, rather than go to work for nine o'clock, I got the bus and went to the university for an eleven o'clock lecture. I was sitting there, in the lecture room, and I thought to myself, 'Why don't I know anybody?' Then suddenly I remembered that I'd finished university and that I was two hours late for work!

**Josh**

I'm studying law in London now, and um, at the end of last term I packed my suitcase as usual, and went to King's Cross Station to catch the train home. I was sitting reading on the train, revising for my exams, and the inspector came to check my ticket. He looked at it and said, 'Thank you, sir. We'll be in Newcastle in about an hour.' And suddenly I thought, 'Newcastle!?! But I don't want to go to Newcastle. My parents live in Plymouth!' You see, when I was a child I lived with my parents in Newcastle, but we moved to Plymouth when I was ten. I couldn't believe it. How could I be so stupid?

**Fiona**

Some time ago I got dressed, ready to go to work. I put on my smart black suit. I'd been working at home the night before – preparing for a very important meeting the next day, and I remembered to put all the right papers into my briefcase. I left home and walked down to the bus stop. Just before I got on the bus, I looked down, and I was still wearing my fluffy, pink bedroom slippers!

## Tapescript 83c

**P = Presenter   A = Alan Buchan**

P  Stories of forgetfulness like these are familiar to many of us and experts say that such cases as Ellen's, Josh's and Fiona's show that loss of memory is not just related to age, but can be caused by our way of life. Professor Alan Buchan, a neuro-psychologist, explains why.

A  One of the problems, these days, is that many companies have far fewer employees and this means that one person often does several jobs. Jobs that before were done by many people are done by a few and they haven't been trained to do this. If you have five things to do at once, you become stressed and forgetful. I think many people in work situations, at a meeting or something, have the experience where they start a sentence and half-way through it, they can't remember what they're talking about, and they can't finish the sentence. It's a terrible feeling – you think you're going mad. I remember one lady who came to me so distressed because at three important meetings in one week, she found herself saying, mid-sentence, 'I'm sorry, I can't remember what I'm talking about.' And, this was a lady in a new job, which involved a lot of travelling. She also had a home and family to look after, *and* she'd recently moved house. She had so *many* things to think about that her brain couldn't cope. It shut down.

P  I can see the problem but what's the solution? How did you help that lady?

A  Well, part of the solution is recognizing the problem. Once we'd talked to this lady about her stressful lifestyle, she realized that she wasn't going crazy, and she felt more relaxed and was able to help herself. But do you know one of the best ways to remember things, even in these days of personal computers and filofaxes?

P  What's that?

A  Well, in fact, it's a notebook – and a pencil of course! At the beginning of every day, write yourself a list of things you have to do, and it gives you a really good feeling when you cross things off the list as you do them! Psychologically, it's *very* satisfying to complete things.

P  Well, there you have it! I hope I can remember how not to forget! Thank you very much indeed Professor … er … er … Oh! Professor Alan Buchan!

## Tapescript 84

a  A  Oh, let's have a break, shall we?
   B  All right. I'm dying for a cuppa.
b  A  My old man isn't at work today.
   B  Why? What's up with him?
   A  He was walking to work yesterday when this guy in a car knocked him over.
   B  Really! Is he OK?
   A  Well, he was very lucky. He just got a few cuts and grazes.
c  A  Can I have one of your fags?
   B  Sure. Help yourself. I've got loads.
   A  Ta! Do *you* want one?
   B  No. I've just put one out.
d  A  Gimme your homework so I can copy it.
   B  No way! You can do it yourself!
e  A  Did you manage to fix the telly?
   B  Kind of. The picture's OK, but the sound isn't quite right.
   A  What's on tonight?
   B  Dunno. Look in the paper.
f  A  What's that stuff called that you use to clean between your teeth?
   B  What do you mean?

A  Oh, you know! It's like string. White.
B  Oh! You mean dental floss.
A  That's it!

# UNIT 12

## Tapescript 85

### The Marriage Proposal

**J = John   M = Moira**

J  Hello, Moira. How are you?
M  I'm fine. How are you?
J  I feel wonderful because we're together again. It's been a long time since our holiday in Paris.
M  Oh, I loved every minute of it. I'll never forget it. Can we go back there next spring?
J  I love you, Moira. Will you marry me and come to Paris with me for our honeymoon?
M  Oh, yes, yes, I will. I love you, too.

## Tapescript 86a

### The Wedding Reception

**A = Adam   B = Beatrice**

A  Are you on your own?
B  No, I'm not. I'm with my husband.
A  How do you know John and Moira, then?
B  I was at university with Moira.
A  Do you like big weddings?
B  I prefer smaller ones.
A  Where did you meet your husband, then?
B  Actually, I met him at a wedding.
A  Why aren't you drinking?
B  Because I'm driving.
A  Er … Have you travelled far to get here?
B  Yes, we have. We flew in from New York yesterday.
A  Hey, why aren't you wearing a hat?
B  I never wear hats.
A  Where are you staying tonight?
B  We're at the *Red Lion*.
A  Oh! Can you give me a lift there?
B  Yes, we can. Are you staying at the *Red Lion*, too?
A  Yes, I am. Will there be enough room in your car?
B  Oh, yes, lots. There won't be a problem.

## Tapescript 86b

### Beatrice talking to her husband

I've just met this really friendly young man. Do you know what he said to me? First he asked me if I was on my own and of course I said that I wasn't, I was with you. Then he asked me how I knew John and Moira and I told him I had been at university with Moira. He asked me if I liked big weddings, and I said no, I preferred smaller ones. Then he asked me where I'd met you, which was a bit of a funny question, so I told him that we'd met at a wedding. He asked me why I wasn't drinking, and I said that it was because I was driving. He asked me if we'd travelled far to get here, so I explained that we'd flown in from New York yesterday.

Then he asked something strange. He asked me why I wasn't wearing a hat, so I said I never wore hats. He then went on to ask me where we were staying tonight, and I told him we were at the *Red Lion*. He asked me if we could give him a lift there, and I said yes. I asked him if he was staying at the *Red Lion*, too, and he said he was. He asked if there would be enough room in our car, and I told him that there wouldn't be a problem.

## Tapescript 87

a  A  He loves living in London.
   B  But he told me he *hated* it!
b  A  He's moving to Canada.
   B  But he told me that he was moving to *Australia*!
c  A  His girlfriend has left him.
   B  But he told me that he'd left *her*!
d  A  He'll be thirty next week.
   B  But he told me he'd be *twenty-one*!
e  A  He went to Amsterdam for his last holiday.
   B  But he told me he'd gone to *Barbados*!
f  A  He can't give up smoking.
   B  But he told me that he'd given up *three years ago*!
g  A  He was given the sack last week.
   B  But he told me he'd been given *promotion*!
h  A  He's fallen in love with a French girl.
   B  Oh! But he told me that he'd fallen in love with *me*!

## Tapescript 88a

**Pauline Peters**

OK. We argue sometimes but not often. Usually we just sit quietly and watch television in the evenings. But sometimes … sometimes we argue about money. We don't have very much because neither of us has a job at the moment, and I get very upset when Peter spends the little we have at the pub or on the horses. He promised to stop drinking but he hasn't stopped. It's worse since he lost his job. OK. We were shouting but we didn't throw a chair at Mr Fish. It … er … it just fell out of the window. And I'm really sorry that we woke the baby. We won't do it again. We love children. We'll babysit for Mr and Mrs Fish anytime if they want to go out.

## Tapescript 88b

**Iris Fish**

Every night it's the same. They argue every night. And we can hear every word they say. During the day it's not so bad because they're both out at work. But in the evenings it's terrible. Usually, they start arguing about which television programme to watch. Then he bangs the door and marches down the road to the pub. Last night he came back really drunk. He was shouting outside his front door. 'Open the door you … er … so and so.' I won't tell you the language he used! But she wouldn't open it, she opened a window instead and threw a plant at him. Tonight she threw a chair at my poor husband. They're so selfish. They don't even care about the baby.

## Tapescript 89a,b   See pages 121–122

## Tapescript 90   See page 123

## Tapescript 91a

a 'Excuse me, can you tell me where the post office is?'
'Sorry, I'm a stranger here myself.'

b 'Ouch! That's my foot!'
'Oh, I'm sorry. I wasn't looking where I was going.'

c 'Er ... Excuse me, what's that creature called?'
'It's a Diplodocus.'
'Pardon?'
'A Diplodocus. D-I-P-L-O-D-O-C-U-S.'
'Er ... Thank you very much.'

d 'I failed my driving test for the sixth time!'
'I am sorry.'

e 'Excuse me! We need to get past. My little boy isn't feeling well.'

f 'Do you want your hearing aid, Grandma?'
'Pardon?'
'I said: *Do you want your hearing aid?*'
'What?'
'DO YOU WANT YOUR HEARING AID?'
'I'm sorry, I can't hear you. I need my hearing aid.'
'Oooh!'

## Tapescript 91b

a Hello, Elana? Hello, again! I don't know what happened. I think we must have been cut off. I'm sorry about that. Never mind. Now, where were we?

b Excuse me! Hello! Excuse me! Excuse me, please! Hi! Yes, please! Can we have another large bottle of fizzy mineral water, please? Thanks.

c Oh, I *am* sorry to hear about that. Of course I understand. We'll go out another time.

d What! You want to go where? And with a bottle of whisky? How old do you think you are? Huh! You can think again!

e Excuse me! I wonder if you could help me. I bought this jumper, and I thought it was medium, but when I got home I saw it was the wrong size. Can I change it?

f Pardon? Could you say that again, please. I didn't understand.

g Excuse me, please! Thank you. Oh! Excuse me, I'm getting off at the next stop. Sorry, I've got a big suitcase.

h Oh, no! Of course, you're vegetarian! I *am* sorry! How awful of me. Don't worry, there are lots of other things for you to eat.

# Grammar Reference

## UNIT 7

### Present Perfect

The same form (*have* + past participle) exists in many European languages, but the uses in English are different. In English the Present Perfect is essentially a *present* tense but it also expresses the effect of past actions and activities on the present.

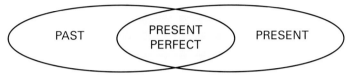

Present Perfect means 'before now'. The Present Perfect does not express *when* an action happened. If we say the exact time, we have to use the Past Simple.

*In my life I **have travelled** to all five continents.*
*I **travelled** round Africa **in 1988**.*

#### • Form

**Positive and negative**

| I<br>We<br>You<br>They | 've<br>haven't | lived in Rome. |
|---|---|---|
| He<br>She | 's<br>hasn't | |

**Question**

| How long have | I<br>we<br>you | known Peter? |
|---|---|---|
| How long has | she<br>he | |

#### • Use

The Present Perfect has three main uses.

1 It expresses an action which began in the past and still continues.
*We've **lived** in the same house for twenty-five years.*
*Peter's **worked** as a teacher since 1991.*
*How long **have** you **known** each other?*
*They've **been** married for twenty years.*

Many languages express this idea with a present tense: 'Peter is a teacher; Peter is a teacher for ten years', but in English the second sentence is wrong.

~~Peter is a teacher for ten years.~~ ✗

*Peter has been a teacher for ten years.* ✔

Note the time expressions that are common with this use. We use *for* with a period of time, and *since* with a point in time.

| for | two years<br>a month<br>a few minutes<br>half an hour<br>ages | since | 1970<br>the end of the lesson<br>August<br>8.00<br>Christmas |
|---|---|---|---|

2 It expresses an experience that happened at some time in one's life. The action is in the past and finished, but the effects of the action are still felt. *When* the action happened is not important.

*I've **been** to the States.* (I still remember.)
*She's **written** poetry, children's stories, and biographies.* (In her writing career)
***Have** you ever **had** an operation?* (At any time in your life up to now)
*How many times **has** he **been** married?* (In his life)

Note the adverbs that are common with this use.

*Have you **ever** been to Australia? I've **never** tried bunjee jumping.*
*I haven't tried sake **before**. It's very nice.*

Note that questions and answers about definite times are expressed in the Past Simple.

*When **did** you **go** to the States?*
***Was** her poetry **published** while she was alive?*
*I **broke** my leg once, but I **didn't** have to stay in hospital.*
*He **met** his second wife in the dry cleaner's.*

3 It expresses a past action that has a present result. The action is usually in the recent past.

*I've **lost** my wallet.* (I haven't got it now.)
*The taxi **hasn't arrived**.* (We're still waiting for it.)
*What **have** you **done** to your lip?* (It's bleeding.)
*Peter **has shaved** his beard off!* (He looks different.)

We often announce news in the Present Perfect, because the speaker is emphasizing the event as a present fact.

***Have** you **heard**? The Prime Minister **has resigned**.*
*Susan's **had** her baby!*
*I've **ruined** the meal. It's burnt.*

Note the adverbs that are common with this use.

*I haven't done my homework **yet**.* (Negative)
*Has the postman been **yet**?* (Question)
*I've **already** done my homework.*
*I've **just** seen some scissors. Now where did I put them?*

Again, details about definite time will be in the Past Simple.

*She **resigned** because she lost a vote of no confidence.*
*She **had** a baby boy this morning. It **was** a difficult birth.*
*I **didn't watch** it carefully enough.*

### Final notes

1 Be careful with *been* and *gone*.
*He's **been** to America.* (= experience – he isn't there now.)
*She's **gone** to America.* (= present result – she's there now.)

2 Compare the following sentences.
  a  *I've **lived** in Paris for six years.* (I still live there.)
     *I **lived** in Paris for six years.* (Now I live somewhere else.)
  b  *Shakespeare **wrote** thirty plays.* (He can't write any more.)
     *I've **written** several books.* (I can still write some more.)
  c  *Have you **seen** Billy this morning?* (It's still morning.)
     *Did you **see** Billy this morning?* (It's the afternoon or evening.)

3 Compare the following right and wrong sentences.

| | RIGHT | WRONG |
|---|---|---|
| a | When did you go to Greece? | * ~~When have you been to Greece?~~ |
| b | I saw him yesterday. | * ~~I have seen him yesterday.~~ |
| c | I've studied English for three years. | * ~~I study English for three years.~~ |
| d | Where did you buy your jumper? | * ~~Where have you bought your jumper?~~ |
| e | I haven't brought my dictionary to class. | * ~~I didn't bring my dictionary to class.~~ |

4 We can see how the Present Perfect refers to indefinite time and the Past Simple refers to definite time by looking at the time expressions used with the different tenses.

| Present Perfect – indefinite | | Past Simple – definite | |
|---|---|---|---|
| I've done it | for a long time. since July. before. recently. | I did it | yesterday. last week. two days ago. at eight o'clock. in 1987. when I was young. for a long time. |
| I've already done it. I haven't done it yet. | | | |

5 American English is different from British English. In American English, the following sentences are correct.

*Did you hear the news? The President resigned!*
*Did you do your homework yet?*
*Your father just called you.*
*I already had breakfast.*

## Multi-word verbs

There are four types of multi-word verbs.

### Type 1

### Verb + particle (no object)

a *He put on his coat and **went out**.*
b *I didn't put enough wood on the fire and it **went out**.*

In a, the verb and particle are used literally. In b, they are used idiomatically. *To go out* means to stop burning.

Examples with literal meaning:
***Sit down**.*
*She **stood up** and **walked out**.*
*Please **go away**.*
*She **walked** right **past** the shop without noticing it.*

Examples with idiomatic meaning:
*The meat has **gone off**. (= go bad)*
*The marriage didn't **work out**. (= succeed)*
*Our plans **fell through**. (= fail)*

### Type 2

### Verb + particle + object (separable)

a *I **put up** the picture.*
b *I **put up** my sister for the night.*

In a, the verb and particle are used literally. In b, they are used idiomatically. *To put up* means to give someone food and a place to sleep usually for the night or a few days.

Type 2 multi-word verbs are separable. The object (noun or pronoun) *can* come between the verb and the particle.

*I **put up** the picture.*      *I **put up** my sister.*
*I **put** the picture **up**.*      *I **put** my sister **up**.*

But if the object is a pronoun, it *always* comes between the verb and the particle.

*I **put** it **up**.*    NOT * I put up it.
*I **put** her **up**.*    NOT * I put up her.

Examples with a literal meaning:
*The waiter **took away** the plates.*
*Don't **throw** it **away**.*
*They're **pulling** that old building **down**.*

Examples with an idiomatic meaning:
*I **put off** the meeting. (= postpone)*
*She **told** her boyfriend **off** for being late. (= be angry with)*
*Don't **let** me **down**. (= disappoint)*

### Type 3

### Verb + particle + object (inseparable)

a *She **came across** the room.*
b *She **came across** an old friend while she was out shopping.*

In a, the verb and particle are used literally. In b, they are used idiomatically. *To come across* means to find by accident.

Type 3 multi-word verbs are inseparable. The object (noun or pronoun) *always* comes after the particle.
NOT *She came an old friend across. or *She came her across.

Examples with a literal meaning:
*I'm **looking for** Jane.*
*They **ran across** the park*
*We **drove past** them.*

Examples with an idiomatic meaning:
*I'll **look after** it for you. (= care for)*
*She **takes after** her father. (= resemble)*
*He never **got over** the death of his wife. (= recover from)*

### Type 4

### Verb + particle + particle

*I **get on** very well **with** my boss.*
*I'm **looking forward to** it.*
*How can you **put up with** that noise?*

Type 4 multi-word verbs are nearly always idiomatic. The object cannot change position. It cannot come before the particles, or between the particles.

NOT *I'm looking forward it to.

# UNIT 8

## Conditionals

There are many different ways of making sentences with *if*. It is important to understand the difference between sentences that express *real* possibilities, and those that express *unreal* situations.

**Real possibilities**
*If it **rains**, we'll stay at home. (if + Present Simple + will)*
*If you've **finished** your work, you **can** go home. (if + Present Perfect + modal auxiliary verb)*
*If you're **feeling** ill, **go** home and **get** into bed. (if + Present Continuous + imperative)*

**Unreal situations**
*You **would understand** me better if you **came** from my country. (would + if + Past Simple)*
*If I **were** rich, I **wouldn't have** any problems. (if + were + would)*
*If I **stopped** smoking, I **could run** faster. (if + Past Simple + modal auxiliary verb)*

There are several patterns which you need to know to understand the variations. Note that a comma is usual when the *if* clause comes first.

### First Conditional

● Form

*If* + Present Simple + *will*

**Positive**
*If I **find** your wallet, **I'll** let you know.*
***We'll** come and see you on Sunday if the weather's good.*

**Negative**
*You **won't** pass the exams if you **don't** revise.*
*If you **lose** your ticket, you **won't** be able to go.*

**Question**

*What will you do if you don't find a job?*
*If there isn't a hotel, where will you stay?*

Note that we do not usually use *will* in the *if* clause.

NOT *If you will leave now, you'll catch the train.
     *If I'll go out tonight, I'll give you a ring.

*If* can be replaced by *unless* (= if … not) or *in case* (= because of the possibility …).
**Unless** *I hear from you, I'll arrive at 8 o'clock.*
*I'll take my umbrella **in case** it rains.*

• **Use**

1  First Conditional sentences express a possible condition and its probable result in the future.

| Condition (*if* clause) | Result (Result clause) |
|---|---|
| *If I find a jumper that suits you,* | *I'll buy it for you.* |
| *If you can do the homework,* | *give me a ring.* |
| *If you can find my purse,* | *I might buy you an ice-cream.* |
| *If you've never been to Wales,* | *you should try to get there one day.* |

2  We can use the First Conditional to express different functions (all of which express a possible condition and a probable result.)
*If you do that again, I'll kill you!* (= a threat)
*Careful! If you touch that, you'll burn yourself!* (= a warning)
*I'll post the letter if you like.* (= an offer)
*If you lend me £100, I'll love you forever.* (= a promise)

## Second conditional

• **Form**

*If + Past Simple + would*

**Positive**

*If I **won** some money, **I'd** go round the world.*
*My father **would** kill me if he **could** see me now.*

**Negative**

*I'd give up my job if I **didn't like** it.*
*If I **saw** a ghost, I **wouldn't** talk to it.*

**Question**

*What **would** you do if you **saw** someone shoplifting?*
*If you **needed** help, who **would** you ask?*

Note that *was* can change to *were* in the condition clause.

| If I / If he | were rich, | I / he | wouldn't have to work. |
|---|---|---|---|

• **Use**

1  We use the Second Conditional to express an unreal situation and its probable result. The situation or condition is improbable, impossible, imaginary, or contrary to known facts.
*If I were the president of my country, I'd increase taxation.* (But it's not very likely that I will ever be the president.)
*If my mother was still alive, she'd be very proud.* (But she's dead.)
*If Ted needed any money, I'd lend it to him.* (But he doesn't need it.)

2  Other modal verbs are possible in the result clause.
*I **could** buy some new clothes if I had some money.*
*If I saved a little every week, I **might** be able to save up for a car.*
*If you wanted that job, you'**d have** to apply very soon.*

3  *If I were you, I'd …* is used to give advice.
**If I were you, I'd** *apologize to her.*
**I'd** *take it easy for a while **if I were you**.*

**First or Second Conditional?**

Both conditionals refer to the present and future. The difference is about probability, not time. It is usually clear which conditional to use. First Conditional sentences are real and possible; Second Conditional sentences express situations that will probably never happen.
*If I lose my job, I'll …* (My company is doing badly. There is a strong possibility of being made redundant.)
*If I lost my job, I'd …* (Redundancy probably won't happen. I'm just speculating.)
*If there is a nuclear war, we'll all …* (Said by a pessimist.)
*If there was a nuclear war, …* (But I don't think it will happen.)

**Zero Conditional**

Zero Conditional sentences refer to 'all time', not just the present or future. They express a situation that is always true. *If* means *when* or *whenever*.
*If you spend over £20 at that supermarket, you get a 5% discount.*

## Time clauses

Conjunctions of time (*when, as soon as, before, until, after*) are not usually followed by will. We use a present tense even though the time reference is future.
*I'll phone you **when I get** home.*
***As soon as** dinner **is** ready, I'll give you a call.*
*Can I have a word with you **before I go**?*
*Wait **until I come** back.*

We can use the Present Perfect if it is important to show that the action in the time clause is finished.
*When I've read the book, I'll lend it to you.*
*I'll go home after I've done the shopping.*

## would

Notice the use of *would* in the following sentences:
*She'd look better with shorter hair.* (= If she cut her hair, she'd look better.)

**would to express preference**

*I'd love a cup of coffee.*
*Where would you like to sit?*
*I'd rather have coffee, please.*
*I'd rather not tell you, if that's all right.*
*What would you rather do, stay in or go out?*

**would to express a request**

*Would you open the door for me?*
*Would you mind lending me a hand?*

# UNIT 9

## Modal verbs (2) *must, could, might, can't*

There is an introduction to modal auxiliary verbs in Unit 4. Modal verbs can express ability, obligation, permission, and request. They can also express the idea of probability, or how certain a situation is.

**Expressing possibility/probability**

1  We use *must* and *can't* to express the logical conclusion of a situation: *must* = logically probable; *can't* = logically improbable. We don't have all the facts, so we are not absolutely sure, but we are pretty certain.
*He's very fit, though he **must be** at least sixty!*
*Suzie **can't have** a ten-year-old daughter! She's only twenty-five herself!*
*Is there no reply? They **must be** in bed. They **can't be** out at this time of night.*
*A walk in this weather! You **must be joking**!*

2　We use **may**/**might** and **could** to express possibility in the present or future. **May**/**Might** + *not* is the negative. *Couldn't* is rare in this use.
*Take your umbrella. It **might rain** later*
*Dave and Beth aren't at home. They **could be** in the pub, I suppose.*
*We **may go** to Greece for our holidays. We haven't decided yet.*
*You know we're going out tonight? Well, I **might not be able** to make it. I **might have to work** late.*

3　We use **will** to express what we believe to be true about the present. We are guessing based on what we know about people and things, their routines, character, and qualities.
*'There's a knock on the door.' 'That**'ll be** the postman. He always calls at this time.'*

## Infinitives

Notice the different infinitives.

### Continuous infinitive

*You must **be joking**!*
*Peter must **be working** late.*
*She **could have been lying** to you.*

### Perfect infinitive to express degrees of probability in the past

*He **must have been** drunk.*
*She **can't have got** home yet.*
*He **might have got** lost.*
*They **could have moved** house.*

### Asking about possibilities

Question forms with the above modal verbs are unusual. We usually use *Do you think …?*
*'**Do you think** she's married?'　'She can't be.'*
*'Where **do you think** he's from?'　'He might be French. He's very handsome.'*
*'**Do you think** they've arrived yet?'　'They may have. Or they might have got stuck in the traffic.'*

## So do I! Neither do I!

Notice how we repeat the auxiliary verbs when we agree or disagree by using *So …/Neither … I*. If there is no auxiliary, use *do/does/did*. Be careful with sentence stress.

| AGREEING | | DISAGREEING | |
|---|---|---|---|
| I like ice-cream. | So do I. | I don't like Mary. | I do. |
| I don't like working. | Neither do I. | I like blue cheese. | I don't. |
| I can swim. | So can I. | I can speak Polish. | I can't. |
| I can't drive. | Neither can I. | I saw Pat yesterday. | I didn't. |
| I'm wearing jeans. | So am I. | We're going now. | We aren't. |
| I went out. | So did I. | I haven't been skiing. | I have. |
| I haven't been to Paris. | Neither have I. | I'm going to have a coffee. | I'm not. |

There are several ways of expressing the same ideas.
*'I like ice-cream.'　'**I do, too.**' / '**Me too.**'*
*'I don't like working.'　'**I don't, either.**' / '**Me neither.**'*

# UNIT 10

## Present Perfect Continuous

Remember the ideas expressed by all continuous forms.

**1　Activity in progress**
*Be quiet! **I'm thinking**.*
*I **was having** a bath when the phone rang.*
*I**'ve been working** since nine o'clock this morning.*

**2　Temporary activity**
*We**'re staying** with friends until we find our own place to live.*
*We**'ve been living** with them for six weeks.*

**3　Possibly incomplete activity**
*I**'m writing** a report. I have to finish it by tomorrow.*
*Who**'s been eating** my sandwich?*

### • Form

**Positive and negative**

| I<br>We<br>You<br>They | 've<br>haven't | been working. |
|---|---|---|
| He<br>She<br>It | 's<br>hasn't | |

**Question**

| How long | have | I<br>you<br>we | been working? |
|---|---|---|---|
| | has | she<br>it | |

### • Use

1　The Present Perfect Continuous expresses an activity which began in the past and is still continuing now.
*I**'ve been learning** English for three years.*
*How long **have** you **been working** here?*

There is sometimes no difference between the Simple and the Continuous.

| *I've played* | |
|---|---|
| *I've been playing* | *the piano since I was a boy.* |

If the Continuous is possible, English has a preference for using it.

The Continuous can sometimes express a temporary activity, and the Simple a permanent state.
*I**'ve been living** in this flat for the past few months. (= temporary)*
*I**'ve lived** here all my life. (= permanent)*

Remember that state verbs rarely take the Continuous.
*I**'ve had** this book for ages.*
*I**'ve always loved** sunny days.*

2　The Present Perfect Continuous expresses a past activity which has caused a present result.
*I**'ve been working** all day. (I'm tired now.)*
***Have** you **been crying**? (Your eyes are red.)*
*Roger**'s been cutting** the grass. (I can smell it.)*

The past activity might be finished or it might not. The context usually makes this clear.
*Look outside the window! It**'s been snowing**! (It has stopped snowing now.)*
*I**'ve been writing** this book for two years. (It still isn't finished.)*
*I'm covered in paint because I**'ve been decorating** the bathroom. (It might be finished or it might not. We don't know.)*

# Present Perfect Simple or Continuous?

1 The Simple expresses a completed action.

*I've **painted** the kitchen, and now I'm doing the bathroom.*

The Continuous expresses an activity over a period, and things that happened during the activity.

*I've got paint in my hair because **I've been decorating.***

2 Think of the verbs that have the idea of a long time, for example, *wait*, *work*, *play*, *try*, *learn*, *rain*. These verbs are often found in the Continuous.

Think of the verbs that *don't* have the idea of a long time, for example *find*, *start*, *buy*, *die*, *lose*, *break*, *stop*. These verbs are more usually found in the Simple.

*I've **been cutting** firewood.* (Perhaps over several hours.)
*I've **cut** my finger.* (One short action.)

3 The Simple expresses a completed action. This is why we use the Simple if the sentence gives a number or quantity, and the Continuous isn't possible.

*I've **been reading** all day. I've **read** ten chapters.*
*She's **been smoking** ever since she arrived. She's **had** ten already.*

## Time expressions

Here are some time expressions often found with certain tenses.

### Past Simple

*I lived in Rome **for six years**.*
*I saw Jack **two days ago**.*
*They met **during the war**.*
*She got married **while she was at university**.*

### Present Perfect

*We've been married **for ten years**.*
*They've been living here **since June**.*
*She hasn't been working **since their baby was born**.*

### Future

*We're going on holiday **for a few days**.*
*The lesson ends **in twenty minutes' time**.*
*I'll be home **in half an hour**.*

### Prepositions with dates, months, years, etc.

| | | | | |
|---|---|---|---|---|
| in | September<br>1965<br>summer<br>the 1920s<br>the twentieth century<br>the holidays<br>the interval | on | Monday<br>Monday morning<br>8 August<br>Christmas Day<br>holiday | at | seven o'clock<br>Christmas<br>the end of May<br>the age of ten<br>tea time |

# UNIT 11

## Questions

Look at the following question words. Notice that *What*, *Which* and *Whose* can combine with a noun, and *How* can combine with an adjective or an adverb.

*What **sort** of music do you like?*
*What **kind** of cigarettes do you smoke?*
*What **size** shoes do you take?*
*What **colour** are your eyes?*
*Which **pen** do you want?*
*Which **way** is it to the station?*
*Whose **book** is this?*
*How **much** do you weigh?*
*How **many** brothers and sisters have you got?*
*How **many times** have you been on a plane?*

*How **much** homework do you get every night?*
*How **tall** are you?*
*How **often** do you go to the cinema?*
*How **long** does it take you to get to school?*

## Indirect questions

1 Indirect questions have the same word order as the positive and there is no *do/does/did*.

> Tom lives in Wimbledon.

> I don't know where Tom lives.

NOT *I don't know ~~where does Tom live~~.

Here are some more expressions that introduce indirect questions.

| *I wonder*<br>*I can't remember*<br>*I've no idea*<br>*I'd like to know*<br>*I'm not sure* | *how long the journey takes.* |
|---|---|

If there is no question word, use *if* or *whether*.

*I don't know **if** I'm coming or not.*
*I wonder **whether** it's going to rain.*

2 We often make direct questions into indirect questions to make them sound 'softer' or more polite.

| *Could you tell me*<br>*Do you know*<br>*Do you happen to know*<br>*Have you any idea*<br>*Do you remember* | *what time the banks close?* |
|---|---|

## Question tags

1 Question tags are very common in spoken English. We use them to keep conversation going by involving listeners and inviting them to participate. The most common patterns are: positive sentence – negative tag, or negative sentence – positive tag.

*You're Jenny, **aren't** you?*
*It **isn't** a very nice day, **is** it?*

2 We repeat the auxiliary verb in the tag. If there is no auxiliary, use *do/does/did*.

*You **haven't** been here before, **have** you?*
*You **can** speak French, **can't** you?*
*We **must** take the dog out, **mustn't** we?*
*She eats meat, **doesn't** she?*
*Banks close at four, **don't** they?*
*You went to bed late, **didn't** you?*

Careful with question tags with *I'm* ...

*I'm late, **aren't** I?* (NOT *~~am't I~~*)

3 Notice the meaning of *yes* and *no* in answer to question tags.

'*You're coming, aren't you?*' '*Yes.*' (= I **am** coming.)
'*No.*' (= I'**m not** coming.)

4 The meaning of a question tag depends on how you say it. If the tag falls, the speaker expects people to agree with him/her.

*Beautiful day, isn't it?*

*It's just the sort of weather for swimming, isn't it?*

*I'm a silly person, aren't I?*

*You don't like my mother, do you?*

If the tag rises, the speaker is asking for confirmation. The speaker thinks he/she knows the answer, but isn't absolutely sure.

*Your name's Abigail, isn't it?*

*You're in advertising, aren't you?*

*You work in the city, don't you?*

5  We can also use question tags with negative sentences to make a polite request for information or help.

*You couldn't lend me your car this evening, could you?*

# UNIT 12

## Reported speech

### Reported statements

1  If the reporting verb is in the past tense (e.g. *said, told*), it is usual for the verb in the reported clause to move 'one tense back'.

present ————————▶ past
present perfect ————▶ past perfect
past ————————————▶ past perfect

'**I'm going**.'   *He said he **was going**.*
'She**'s passed** her exams.'   *He told me she **had passed** her exams.*
'My father **died** when I was six.'   *She said her father **had died** when she was six.*

2  If the reporting verb is in the present tense (e.g. *says, asks*), there is no tense change.
'The train **will be** late.'   *He says the train **will be** late.*
'I **come** from Spain.'   *She says she **comes** from Spain.*

3  The 'one tense back' rule does have exceptions. If the reported speech is about something that is still true, the tense remains the same.
Rainforests **are being destroyed**.   *She told him that rainforests **are being destroyed**.*
'I **hate** football.'   *I told him I **hate** football.*

4  The 'one tense back' rule also applies to reported thoughts and feelings.
*I thought she **was** married, but she isn't.*
*I didn't know he **was** a teacher. I thought he **worked** in a bank.*
*I forgot you **were** coming. Never mind. Come in.*
*I hoped you **would** ring.*

5  Some modal verbs change.

can ————————▶ could
will ————————▶ would
may ————————▶ might

'She **can** type well.'   *He told me she **could/can** type well.*
'**I'll** help you.'   *She said she**'d** help me.*
'I **may** come.'   *She said she **might** come.*

Other modal verbs don't change.
'You **should** go to bed.'   *He told me I **should** go to bed.*
'It **might** rain.'   *She said she thought it **might** rain.*

*Must* can stay as *must*, or it can change to *had to*.
'I **must** go!'   *He said he **must/had to** go.*

6  In more formal situations, we can use *that* after the reporting verb.
*He told her (that) he would be home late.*
*She said (that) sales were down on last year.*

7  There are many reporting verbs.

We rarely use *say* with an indirect object (i.e. the person spoken to).
*She said she was going.*
NOT *~~She said to me she was going.~~*

*Tell* is always used with an indirect object in reported speech.

| | | |
|---|---|---|
| *She told* | *me*<br>*the doctor*<br>*us*<br>*her husband* | *the news.* |

Many verbs are more descriptive than *say* and *tell*, for example, *explain, interrupt, demand, insist, admit, complain, warn*.

Sometimes we report the idea, rather than the actual words.
'I'll lend you some money.'   *He offered to lend me some money.*
'I won't help you.'   *She refused to help me.*

### Reported questions

1  The word order in reported questions is different in reported speech. There is no inversion of subject and auxiliary verb, and there is no *do/does/did*. This is similar to indirect questions.
'Why have you come here?'   *I asked her why she had come here.*
'What time is it?'   *He wants to know what time it is.*
'Where do you live?'   *She asked me where I lived.*

**Note**
We do not use a question mark in a reported question.
We do not use *say* in reported questions.

He said, ' How old are you?'   *He asked me how old I am.*

2  If there is no question word, use *if* or *whether*.

| | | |
|---|---|---|
| *She wants to know* | *whether*<br>*if* | *she should wear a dress.* |

### Reported commands, requests, etc.

1  Reported commands, requests, offers and advice are formed with a verb + person + *to* + infinitive.
*They **told us to** go away.*
*We **offered to take them** to the airport.*
*He **urged the miners to** go back to work.*
*She **persuaded me to** have my hair cut.*
*I **advised the Prime Minister to** leave immediately.*

**Note**
*say* is not possible. Use *ask … to* or *told … to*, etc.

2  Notice the negative command. Use *not* before *to*.
*He told me **not to tell** anyone.*
*The police warned people **not to go** out.*

3  Notice we use *tell* for both reported statements and reported commands, but the form is different.

**Reported statements**
*He told me that he was going.*
*They told us that they were going abroad.*
*She told them what had been happening.*

**Reported commands**
*He told me to keep still.*
*The police told people to move on.*
*My parents told me to tidy my room.*

4  We use *ask* for both reported commands and reported questions, but the form is different.

**Reported commands**
*I was asked to attend the interview.*
*He asked me to open my suitcase.*
*She asked me not to smoke.*

**Reported questions**
*He asked me what I did for a living.*
*I asked her how much the rent was.*
*She asked me why I had come.*

# Appendix 1

## Irregular verbs

| Base form | Past Simple | Past Participle |
|---|---|---|
| be | was/were | been |
| beat | beat | beaten |
| become | became | become |
| begin | began | begun |
| bend | bent | bent |
| bite | bit | bitten |
| blow | blew | blown |
| break | broke | broken |
| bring | brought | brought |
| build | built | built |
| burn | burned/burnt | burned/burnt |
| burst | burst | burst |
| buy | bought | bought |
| can | could | been able |
| catch | caught | caught |
| choose | chose | chosen |
| come | came | come |
| cost | cost | cost |
| cut | cut | cut |
| dig | dug | dug |
| do | did | done |
| draw | drew | drawn |
| dream | dreamed/dreamt | dreamed/dreamt |
| drink | drank | drunk |
| drive | drove | driven |
| eat | ate | eaten |
| fall | fell | fallen |
| feed | fed | fed |
| feel | felt | felt |
| fight | fought | fought |
| find | found | found |
| fly | flew | flown |
| forget | forgot | forgotten |
| forgive | forgave | forgiven |
| freeze | froze | frozen |
| get | got | got |
| give | gave | given |
| go | went | gone/been |
| grow | grew | grown |
| hang | hanged/hung | hanged/hung |
| have | had | had |
| hear | heard | heard |
| hide | hid | hidden |
| hit | hit | hit |
| hold | held | held |
| hurt | hurt | hurt |
| keep | kept | kept |
| kneel | knelt | knelt |
| know | knew | known |
| lay | laid | laid |
| lead | led | led |
| learn | learned/learnt | learned/learnt |
| leave | left | left |
| lend | lent | lent |

| Base form | Past Simple | Past Participle |
|---|---|---|
| let | let | let |
| lie | lay | lain |
| light | lit | lit |
| lose | lost | lost |
| make | made | made |
| mean | meant | meant |
| meet | met | met |
| must | had to | had to |
| pay | paid | paid |
| put | put | put |
| read /ri:d/ | read /red/ | read /red/ |
| ride | rode | ridden |
| ring | rang | rung |
| rise | rose | risen |
| run | ran | run |
| say | said | said |
| see | saw | seen |
| sell | sold | sold |
| send | sent | sent |
| set | set | set |
| shake | shook | shaken |
| shine | shone | shone |
| shoot | shot | shot |
| show | showed | shown |
| shut | shut | shut |
| sing | sang | sung |
| sink | sank | sunk |
| sit | sat | sat |
| sleep | slept | slept |
| slide | slid | slid |
| smell | smelled/smelt | smelled/smelt |
| speak | spoke | spoken |
| spend | spent | spent |
| spill | spilled/spilt | spilled/spilt |
| spoil | spoiled/spoilt | spoiled/spoilt |
| stand | stood | stood |
| steal | stole | stolen |
| stick | stuck | stuck |
| swim | swam | swum |
| take | took | taken |
| teach | taught | taught |
| tear | tore | torn |
| tell | told | told |
| think | thought | thought |
| throw | threw | thrown |
| understand | understood | understood |
| wake | woke | woken |
| wear | wore | worn |
| win | won | won |
| write | wrote | written |

# Appendix 2

## Verb patterns

### Verbs + -ing

| Verbs + -ing | |
|---|---|
| like<br>love<br>adore<br>enjoy<br>prefer<br>hate<br>can't stand<br>don't mind<br>finish<br>look forward to | doing<br>cooking<br>sightseeing |

**Note**

**Like, love, adore, prefer, hate** are sometimes used with *to* but *-ing* is more usual and more general in meaning.
*I like cooking.*
*I like to cook beef on Sundays.*

### Verbs + to + infinitive

| Verbs + to + infinitive | |
|---|---|
| agree<br>choose<br>dare<br>decide<br>expect<br>forget<br>help<br>hope<br>learn<br>manage<br>need<br>offer<br>promise<br>refuse<br>seem<br>want<br>would like<br>would love<br>would prefer<br>would hate | to do<br><br>to come<br><br>to cook |

**Notes**

1 **Help** and **dare** can be used without *to*.
   *We helped tidy the kitchen.*
   *They didn't dare disagree with him.*
2 **Have to** for obligation
   *I have to wear a uniform.*
3 **Used to** for past habits.
   *I used to smoke but I gave up last year.*

### Verbs + somebody + to + infinitive

| Verbs + somebody + to + infinitive | | |
|---|---|---|
| advise<br>allow<br>ask<br>beg<br>encourage<br>expect<br>help<br>need<br>invite<br>order<br>remind<br>tell<br>want<br>warn (+ not)<br>would like<br>would love<br>would prefer<br>would hate | me<br><br><br>him<br><br>them<br><br>someone | to do<br><br>to go<br><br>to come |

### Verbs + somebody + infinitive (no to)

| Verbs + somebody + infinitive (no *to*) | | |
|---|---|---|
| let<br>make<br>help | her<br>us | do |

**Notes**

1 *To* is used with **make** in the passive.
   *We were made to work hard.*
2 **Let** cannot be used in the passive. **Allowed to** is used instead.
   *She was allowed to leave.*

### Verbs + -ing or to + infinitive (with no change in meaning)

| Verbs + -ing or to + infinitive (with no change in meaning) | |
|---|---|
| begin<br>start<br>continue | raining<br>to rain |

### Verbs + -ing or to + infinitive (with a change in meaning)

| Verbs + -ing or to + infinitive (with a change in meaning) | |
|---|---|
| remember<br>stop<br>try | doing<br>to do |

**Notes**

1 *I remember posting the letter.*
   = I have a memory now of a past action: *posting the letter.*
   *I remembered to post the letter.*
   = I reminded myself to post the letter.
2 *I stopped smoking.*
   = I gave up the habit.
   *I stopped to smoke.*
   = I stopped doing something else in order to have a cigarette.
3 *I tried to sleep.*
   = I wanted to sleep but it was difficult.
   *I tried counting sheep and taking sleeping pills.*
   = these were possible ways of getting to sleep.

# Index

## An index of grammatical items and functional areas

(SB 1 = Student's Book Unit 1; WB 3 = Workbook Unit 3; p 2 = page 2)

# Acknowledgements

The authors would like to thank all the staff at Oxford University Press, especially the editor of this book, Elana Katz, for their help, encouragement and dedication throughout the writing of the series. We are deeply indebted to them.

The publishers and authors are very grateful to the following teachers and institutions for reading and/or piloting the manuscript, and for providing invaluable comment and feedback on the course:

Alex Boulton               Paula Jullian
Henny Burke                David Massey
Antonio Marcelino Campo    Paul Packer
Anna Gawrys-Stosio         Jeremy Page
John Golding               Stephanie Richards
Bernie Hayden              Nina Rosa da Silva
Felicity Henderson         Ricardo Sili da Silva
Amanda Jeffries            Russell Stannard
Heather Jones              Sylvia Wheeldon

Akcent Language School, Prague; Aximedia Idiomas, Madrid; The Bell School, Prague; British School of Verona; CLM Bell, Riva del Garda TN; CLM Bell, Trento; EFIP Groupement des Chambres de Commerce et d'Industrie de Castres et de Mazamet; English Language Centre, Ferrara; The 'English Plus' Director and teaching staff at the Colchester English Study Centre; Escola d'Idiomes Moderns, Universitat de Barcelona; The Institute of English, University of Bari; Instituto de Idiomas, Universidad de Navarra, Pamplona; International House, Budapest; International House, Livorno; International House, London; The Oxford Academy; Richard Language College, Bournemouth; Southbourne School of English, Bournemouth; Universidad de los Andes, Santiago.

The authors and publisher are grateful to those who have given permission to reproduce the following extracts and adaptations of copyright material:

p 15   Adapted from 'The happiest person in Britain', The Daily Mail, © The Daily Mail/Solo Syndication, by permission.
p 42   Extract from 'Oxford Wordpower Dictionary', © Oxford University Press.
p 60   Adapted from 'English food: bad taste?', © Focus.
p 70   Taken from ' The modern servant', The Daily Mail, © The Daily Mail/Solo Syndication, by permission.
p 80   Adapted from 'Who wants to be a millionaire?' by Martin Plimmer, SHE Magazine, © National Magazine Company.
p 92   Adapted from 'The Man Who Planted Trees', by Jean Giono, with kind permission of Peter Owen Publishers, London.
p 96   From 'Here Endeth the Lessons', © The Sun.
p 100  Extract from 'Here Have One of Mine', © The Telegraph plc, London, 1994.
p 123  From 'Funeral Blues', Collected Poems by WH Auden edited by Edward Mendelson, with kind permission of Publishers Faber and Faber Ltd.
p 135  'Who wants to be a millionaire?' (Cole Porter), © 1956 Buxton Hill Music Corp, USA and Warner Chappell Music Ltd, London W1Y 3FA, reproduced by kind permisssion of International Music Publications Ltd.

Every endeavour has been made to identify the sources of all material used. The publisher apologizes for any omissions.

**Illustrations by:**
Richard Allen pp 92, 93
Stephan Chabluk pp 64, 67, 74
Nicky Cooney pp 10, 29, 42, 103, 116, 120
Paul Dickinson pp 32, 33
Sue Faulks/Eikon Ltd pp 17, 18, 46
Rosamund Fowler pp 12, 28, 44, 63, 111
Gay Galsworthy p 37
Clive Goodyer pp 22, 80, 91
Hardlines pp 22, 36, 50, 83
Gordon Hendry  p 146
Peter Hudspith pp 39, 72, 75, 106
Conny Jude p 14
Ian Kellas pp  6, 15, 38, 45, 55, 65, 77, 107, 125
Frances Lloyd pp 8, 48, 88, 89
Andrew Morris pp 40, 41, 85, 95, 113
Tracy Rich pp 24, 26, 123
Sue Sheilds pp 121, 122
Margaret Wellbank pp 24, 26, 56, 76, 96, 116, 117

**Handwriting by:**  Kathy Baxendale

**Studio photography by:**  Mark Mason pp 8, 13, 29, 43, 101, 102

**Location Photography by:**
Emily Anderson pp 23, 37, 47, 52, 53, 57, 65, 73, 76, 77, 96, 107, 118, 119
Christine Kelly p 78
Norman McBeath pp 17, 35, 104
John Walmsley pp 16, 124

The publishers would like to thank the following for their permission to reproduce photographs and other copyright material:

Ace Photo Library p 9 (A Mauritius)
All Action Pictures p 81 (pools win)
The Ancient Art and Architecture Collection p 7 (statue)
BBC Photo Library pp 20 (caravan), 21 (portrait)
Madeleine Black p 66
The Anthony Blake Photo Library pp 7 (sushi), 60 (meat pie, Rosenfeld – rosemary), 61 (Tim Imrie)
The Bridgeman Art Library p 29 Guernica 1937 by Pablo Picasso © Succession Picasso/DACS 1996
Derek Cattani p 104 (royalist)
Verity Cooke and family p 88
The Mary Evans Picture Library pp 6 (printing), 7 (Lincoln)
Hulton Deutsch p 31 (Picasso and Joplin)
The Image Bank pp 49 (Bokelberg – flowers), 95 (J Alvarez – man)
Impact Photos pp 15 (C Cormack – old man), 34 (E Houssein – outdoor café, P Cavendish – indoor café, S Fear – old men), 54 (G Sweeney)
Life File pp 51 (E Lee – cuckoo clock), 114 (K Curtis – 'Ellen')
Little Boats Model Agency p 56
Billie Love Historical Collection p 37 (schoolroom)
Magnum Photo Library p 83 (C Steele–Perkins – meals on wheels)
Mousetrap Productions p 30 (St Martin's and cast)
Network Photo Library pp 19 (B Lewis – whisky and sorting post), 51 (W Buss – Madrid), 62 (G Sioen/Rapho – NY Manhattan), 68 (M Goldwater), 83 (G Mendel – homeless person), 115 (H Salvadori – commuters)
Oxford Photo Library p 95 (C Andrews – skyline)
Popperfoto p 108 (Madame Tussaud)
Rex Features pp 20 (portrait), 81 (A Books – lottery win)
Liz and John Soars p 26
Solo Syndication/Mail Newspapers pp 70, 71
Frank Spooner pp 100 (Gamma), 108 (A Berg – Bill Clinton, Gamma – The Beatles), 112 (old man)
Tony Stone Images pp 6 (Olympics), 10 (F Ivaldi), 11 (T Beddow – sunbathers, M Kezar – harvesters), 15 (P Tweedie – teenager, D Stewart – man with glasses, V Oliver – old lady, K Fisher – young woman and man with moustache), 34 (B Ayres – businesswoman), 49 (H Grey – men embracing), 51 (Venice, AB Wadham – David, A Smith – Big Ben, T Craddock – Belgian Lace), 57 (P Webster – Indian food), 62 (D Hughes – London view, A Sotirou – NY café), 98 (Dale Durfee), 115 (J Garrett – opera house)
Topham Picture Source pp 30 (portrait), 69, 108 (Queen Victoria)
The Times p 9 (Masthead)
John Walmsley Photo Library pp 34 (neighbours), 49 (arranging to meet), 74, 114 ('Josh' and 'Fiona')
Zefa Photo Library pp 19 (long hair), 49 (Mugshots – men shaking hands), 51 (Munich, Eiffel Tower, and Pisa), 62 (Oxford St), 83 (classroom), 86, 109, 111, 112 (Earth), 113 (Dolphin)

We would also like to thank the following for their help:
Eurostar, Waterloo; Joel and Son Fabrics; Little Boats Model Agency; Oxford Tourist Information office

Oxford University Press
Great Clarendon Street, Oxford OX2 6DP

Oxford   New York
Athens  Auckland  Bangkok  Bogota  Bombay
Buenos Aires  Calcutta  Cape Town  Dar es Salaam
Delhi  Florence  Hong Kong  Istanbul  Karachi
Kuala Lumpur  Madras  Madrid  Melbourne
Mexico City  Nairobi  Paris  Singapore
Taipei  Tokyo  Toronto  Warsaw

and associated companies in
Berlin  Ibadan

OXFORD and OXFORD ENGLISH are trade marks of Oxford University Press

ISBN 0 19 470223 5   Complete Edition
ISBN 0 19 435734 1   Student's Book B
ISBN 0 19 435733 3   Student's Book A

© Oxford University Press 1996

First published 1996
Second impression 1997

**No unauthorized photocopying**

Printed in Hong Kong